GOD GIVES
THE LAND

Story Bible Series, Book 3

GOD GIVES THE LAND

Stories of God and His People:
Joshua, Judges, and Ruth

Retold by Eve B. MacMaster

Illustrated by James Converse

HERALD PRESS
Scottdale, Pennsylvania
Kitchener, Ontario
1983

Library of Congress Cataloging in Publication Data

MacMaster, Eve, 1942-
  God gives the land.

  (Story Bible series; bk. 3)
  Summary: A collection of thirty-five Bible stories
from the Book of Joshua, Judges, and Ruth.
  1. Bible stories, English—O.T. Joshua.   2. Bible
stories, English—O.T. Judges.   3. Bible stories,
English—O.T. Ruth. [1. Bible stories—O.T. Joshua.
2. O.T. Judges.   3. Bible Stories—O.T.
Ruth] I. Converse, James.   II. Bible. O.T. Joshua.
God gives the land.   III. Bible. O.T. Judges. God
gives the land.   IV. Bible. O.T. Ruth. God gives
the land.   V. Title.   VI. Series.

BS551.2.M2958   1983   222'.209505   83-182
ISBN 0-8361-3332-3 (pbk.)

GOD GIVES THE LAND
Copyright © 1983 by Herald Press, Scottdale, Pa. 15683
  Published simultaneously in Canada by Herald Press,
  Kitchener, Ont. N2G 4M5
Library of Congress Catalog Card Number: 83-182
International Standard Book Number: 0-8361-3332-3
Printed in the United States of America
Design: Alice B. Shetler

83 84 85 86 87 88 89 10 9 8 7 6 5 4 3 2 1

A Note to the Reader

God's Gives the Land is Book 3 of the Herald Press Story Bible Series.

As you read these stories, I hope you feel some of the joy and excitement I have felt in retelling them.

The series began several years ago when I tried to find a Bible storybook to read to my three young children. When I couldn't find one that was complete, faithful to the original, and fun to read, I decided to try to write one myself. I've been busy ever since.

These stories are meant to be an introduction to the wonders of the Bible, the world's favorite book, not a substitute for it. Although it is more complete than other Bible storybooks, it is still a simplification. Hopefully, it will help bridge the gap between our world and the world of the Bible and lead its readers to the original.

The Bible was first written centuries ago in the Hebrew and Greek languages to tell about God's actions in human history. It has been translated and retold in every generation, because people everywhere want to know what God is like.

The Bible says that God is a person. As we meet God—the main character in the Bible—we meet someone who is loving, merciful, and just. We learn that he has a sense of humor and enjoys a good story!

The first book in the series, *God's Family*, is a retelling of Genesis, the first book of the Bible. It tells how God created the world and everything in it. God's creation was good, but the people that God made rebelled against him. Instead of giving up on them, God decided to teach them how he wanted them to live. He began to do this by choosing one family from all the families on earth—the family of Abraham.

The second book in the series is *God Rescues His People*. It tells how God's family became the nation of Israel, a small nation with a great God. God picked Moses to lead his people out of slavery, teach them his ways, and bring them to the edge of the Promised Land.

This book, *God Gives the Land*, tells how God kept the promises he made to Abraham and Moses. He brings the nation of Israel into the land, defeats their enemies, and gives them everything they need. When the people find themselves in deep trouble, God sends saviors—the judges. In the story of Ruth, we learn how God works in the lives of people who live as God wants them to live.

Retelling the whole Bible would be impossible without the help and encouragement I have received from some of God's people.

Special thanks to my advisory committee, who read the manuscript at an early stage: Bible professors George R. Brunk III, Ronald D. Guengerich, G. Irvin Lehman, and Kenneth Seitz; childhood curriculum and librarian specialists Elsie E. Lehman and A. Arlene Bumbaugh; and book marketing specialist Angie B. Williams.

Appreciation to Paul M. Schrock, book editor at Herald Press, for his valued advice; to Sam, Tom, and Sarah MacMaster, for their special testing; to Richard MacMaster, for his constant support.

In the spirit of the book of Ruth, this book is dedicated to my parents, Quentin and Ruth Bowers, for their loving-kindness through the years.

Eve MacMaster
Bridgewater, Virginia
All Saints' Day, 1982

Contents

A Redeemer for Naomi

God Gives
the Land

Waiting for Orders

Joshua 1

LONG ago on a day early in spring, the people of Israel camped outside the land of Canaan at a place called Shittim. Herds of cattle and flocks of sheep and goats nibbled on the grass all around the camp, waiting. Children played on the ground between the black goat-hair tents, waiting. Men and women stood around talking in front of the tents, waiting.

They were used to waiting. Forty years ago they had escaped from Egypt, where they had been slaves. The Lord their God had rescued them. He had given them a leader, Moses, to bring them out of Egypt and across the great wilderness to this place.

The Israelites were God's special people. He had chosen them, not because they were better than anyone else, but just because he loved them. The Lord promised to be their God if they would worship him and obey him. He gave the Ten Commandments and other instructions so his people would know how to live.

After God's people crossed the wilderness, the Lord took Moses up to the top of a mountain to show him the land of Canaan. This was the land he was going to give to his people, as he had promised their ancestors.

Then Moses died on the mountain, and the Lord gave the people a new leader, Moses' helper, Joshua. Joshua would be the one to lead the people into the Promised Land.

So here they were, at the edge of the land, waiting.

Finally, Joshua had a message from the Lord. It was time to move!

He told the leaders of the twelve tribes of Israel what the Lord had said: "Get ready," the Lord told Joshua. "It's time for you and all the people of Israel to cross the Jordan River and enter the land! I'm giving it all to you, from the wilderness in the south to the mountains in the north, from the wide Euphrates River to the Great Western Sea!

"Be strong and brave, Joshua! I've chosen you to lead my people. As long as you live, no one will defeat you, for I'll be with you, as I was with Moses. I'll fight Israel's battles, and I'll give you the land.

"Obey the instructions which I have given you, Joshua. Read and study them every day. Don't worry, for I am your God, and I am with you wherever you go. I will never leave you."

Then Joshua gave special orders to the leaders of two and a half of the tribes. "You tribes of Reuben and Gad and half the tribe of Manasseh already have your land," he said. "The Lord con-

quered the land on this side of the river and gave it to you before Moses died. Now leave your wives and children here and cross the Jordan River with us. Bring your swords and spears, for we need you to fight with us. After we take the land on the other side of the river, you can come back here and settle."

"We'll do whatever you tell us," they answered, "and we'll go wherever you send us. We'll obey you just as we obeyed Moses. May the Lord our God be with you as he was with Moses!"

Then Joshua spoke to the leaders of the tribes of Simeon, Judah, Issachar, Zebulun, Benjamin, Dan, Naphtali, Asher, Ephraim, and the other half of the tribe of Manasseh. "Go through the camp and tell the people to prepare food for a journey," he told them. "In a few days we'll cross the River Jordan and take the land the Lord is giving to us!"

The Secret of the Scarlet Cord

Joshua 2

WHEN the Israelites came into the land of Canaan, they found many different groups of people living there. The land was divided into city-states, each ruled by its own king.

Before this, the Egyptians ruled over Canaan, and after this, people from the north were in control. But at this time in history, no one great power was in charge. The Israelites fought many battles all over Canaan, and it took many years to conquer the land.

The word "Canaan" comes from a word for

purple. The land of Canaan was named after the purple dye which the Canaanites used to color their wool. They traded the wool for copper from Cyprus and carved ivory from Egypt. The clever Canaanites were also the first people in the world to invent an alphabet.

The Canaanites lived in large cities surrounded by thick, high walls. They had horses and chariots to protect themselves from invaders.

But the people of Canaan worshiped other gods. The Lord wanted to punish them, drive them out, and give their land to the Israelites. He wanted the Israelites to destroy the pagan altars and images. He wanted them to show the world how to live and worship.

Joshua chose two brave young men and ordered them to go secretly and explore the land of Canaan, especially the city of Jericho.

Jericho lay only a few miles away from the Israelite camp, on the other side of the Jordan. It stood between the Jordan Valley and the hill country.

The two spies left the camp and walked a few miles across the open country. When they came to the river, they looked around until they found a place where they could wade across.

They walked a few more miles across the hot valley. Then they arrived at Jericho. The two young men slipped through the city gate, the only opening in the great walls. After exploring the city, they found a place to spend the night, a house on the city wall run by a woman named Rahab.

But someone saw the Israelites and reported them to the king of Jericho. He sent a search party to get them.

The king's men knocked at Rahab's door. Before she answered, she hid her visitors under some stalks of flax that were piled on the flat roof of her house to dry.

"Those men who are staying with you are spies!" the king's men said to her. "Turn them over to us!"

"Some men were here earlier," Rahab answered, "but I didn't know who they were. They left a few minutes ago, at sundown, just before the city gate was closed for the night. I have no idea where they went. If you hurry, maybe you can catch them!"

The search party left, and Rahab rushed up to the roof of her house. The spies crawled from their hiding place under the stalks of flax.

"Everyone here is terrified of you!" Rahab told them. "We heard how your God dried up the sea in front of you as you left Egypt! He defeated the kings on the other side of the Jordan! As soon as we heard these things, we lost our courage. I believe the Lord your God is the God of heaven and earth! I know he has given you this land, and that's why I've taken care of you. Promise me, in the name of the Lord, that you'll take care of my family. Spare their lives when you take our city!"

"We promise," they answered. "We won't hurt your family. If you don't tell anyone what we're doing here, we'll protect you as you have protected us!"

Then Rahab fastened a rope in a window of her house. Since the house was built into the side of the wall, the spies could slide down the rope and get safely out of the locked city without being seen.

"Head for the hills," she said, "and hide until the king's men give up looking for you."

"We'll be back," said the spies, "but before that, here's what you must do. Tie a scarlet cord in this same window, and let it hang out. Bring your whole family inside the house and keep them here when we come back to Jericho. We'll tell our people to look for the red-colored cord. They won't hurt the people in the house where it is hanging out."

"Just as you say," she answered.

Then the spies climbed down the rope and sneaked away from Jericho in the dark.

After they left, Rahab tied a scarlet cord to the window.

The king's men looked for the spies all along the road, but they had gone in the opposite direction. After three days the search party gave up and went back to Jericho. The two Israelites came down from the hills and made their way safely back to the camp.

They told Joshua everything that had happened.

"The Lord has given us the whole country!" they reported. "Everyone there is already terrified of us!"

3

Crossing the Jordan

Joshua 3—5

AFTER the spies came back from Jericho, Joshua told the people to take down their tents and walk to the Jordan River. When the Israelites saw the fast-moving water overflowing the river banks, they worried about how they would cross. How could thousands of people with all their baggage and little children and animals ever get across to the other side? Not even a strong man could wade through that flood!

They camped beside the Jordan River for three days, preparing themselves for something—they didn't know what—that the Lord was going to do for them.

On the third day they saw Joshua moving toward the river. The priests were with him, and they were carrying the ark of the covenant!

The ark was a large wooden box covered with gold. Inside the ark were the stone tablets of the law. These tablets were the sign of the special agreement, called the covenant, which the Lord had made with his people.

The Israelites had no images, no carved figures or idols like other nations. Their God was invisible. But the ark reminded them that the Lord was with them.

On the solid gold lid of the ark were two golden figures of cherubs. These winged creatures guarded God's throne. The lid of the ark was the footstool of the invisible God's invisible throne.

"Get ready!" cried Joshua. "Today the Lord will do a great miracle among us! You'll see that the living God, the ruler of the whole earth, is with us! You'll see how he's going to drive the Canaanites out of this land!"

Then he ordered the people, "Follow the ark of the covenant!"

The priests took the ark upon their shoulders and marched toward the river. The rest of the people followed them, keeping their distance from the ark. As soon as the priests stepped into the water, something wonderful happened. The water stopped flowing!

Far away, up the river, the water dammed up into a great pile. Far below, it ran on down to the Salt Sea, leaving dry ground and uncovering the rocks at the bottom of the riverbed.

The priests carried the ark down to the middle of the dry riverbed and stood with it on their shoulders while the men, women, and children of Israel crossed the river on dry ground!

After all the people and their belongings were safely across, the Lord told Joshua to choose twelve men, one from each of the tribes of Israel.

"Go down to the river where the priests are standing with the ark," Joshua told them. "Bring back twelve large stones. When we camp tonight, we'll set them up as a monument to remind us what the Lord has done here today!"

The twelve men went into the middle of the dry riverbed, lifted twelve heavy stones onto their shoulders, and carried them out.

Then Joshua told the priests to come out of the river.

As soon as they put their feet on the bank, water began flowing down from upstream! Soon the Jordan was flooding its banks again.

The Israelites were safely across in the land of Canaan, and their feet weren't even wet!

They camped at Gilgal, a few miles west of the river. There Joshua arranged the twelve stones in a circle.

"In the future these stones will help our people remember what happened today," he said. "When your children see these stones they will ask, 'What do these stones mean?' Then you can tell them that the Lord your God dried up the water of the Jordan River in front of the ark, so you could cross over. He worked this miracle so everyone on earth will know how mighty he is!"

4

How the Walls of Jericho Fell Down

Joshua 5—6

NEWS was spreading through the land of Canaan. The Lord had dried up the Jordan River for the Israelites! What terrible thing would happen next? The people of Jericho were so frightened that they shut their city up tight. They locked the gates and guarded the walls to keep the invaders out. No one could go in or out of the city.

Joshua knew that they must take the city of Jericho first, but he wasn't sure how to do it. He went out to take a look for himself.

As Joshua came near the city, he suddenly saw a man standing in front of him. The man was holding a sharp sword in his outstretched hand.

Joshua walked up to him and asked, "Are you with us or with our enemies?"

"I have come as the commander of the army of the Lord!" answered the man.

Then Joshua bowed down to the ground and said, "I am your servant. What is your command?"

"Take off your sandals," said the commander of the Lord's army. "You are standing on holy ground."

Joshua did as he was told, for this was an angel, a messenger from the Lord!

Then the Lord told Joshua how to conquer the city of Jericho, and Joshua went back to the camp at Gilgal.

He lined up the priests and soldiers in marching order. First came the men of Reuben, Gad, and eastern Manasseh. Then came seven priests carrying seven trumpets made of rams' horns. Behind them came the ark of the covenant, carried on the shoulders of other priests. Finally came the rest of the soldiers.

"Don't shout," said Joshua. "Don't say a word or make a sound until I give the order. Now forward march around the city!"

The strange parade of priests and soldiers went to Jericho and marched around the city walls once, with the golden box of the ark of the covenant in the middle of them. As they marched, the priests blew long, loud blasts on their trumpets. Then they all returned to camp.

The next day they lined up in the same order and marched around Jericho again. Again they returned to camp.

They repeated this parade the third day and the fourth and the fifth and the sixth. Each day the people of Jericho watched from the top of the walls and through their windows. What did the strange procession mean? Nothing seemed to be happening—or was it?

On the seventh day the Israelites got up early and went to the city for the last time. This day they marched around the walls of Jericho seven

times. Each time they passed Rahab's house, they saw the scarlet cord hanging from the window.

As they marched, the priests blew the trumpets. After the seventh time around, they all stood still. Even the trumpets were silent.

Joshua told the army, "The Lord has won the battle! The city and everything in it belong to him, so don't take anything for yourselves. If you do, you'll bring trouble to all of us! Destroy everything as an offering to the Lord! Only Rahab and her family are to be spared. Don't take a thing, for it all belongs to the Lord."

Then Joshua cried, "Shout! The Lord has given you the city!"

The priests blew the trumpets and the soldiers shouted a mighty war cry, and the walls of Jericho trembled and shook and fell down!

The soldiers climbed over the rubble of the walls and entered the city, destroying everything in all the houses, both people and animals. The only survivors were the people in the house with the Scarlet cord.

"Go get Rahab!" said Joshua to the two men who had acted as spies. "Take her and her family to a safe place, as you promised."

They went to Rahab's house and found her waiting inside with her whole family. They brought her out with her father and mother and brothers and sisters and took them all to a safe place near the Israelite camp.

They brought out the silver and gold and the bronze and iron things to give to the Lord. Then they set fire to the city and burned it to the ground, along with everything and everybody in it.

Jericho was destroyed, and all its people were dead—all but Rahab and her family. They were safe because Rahab trusted the Lord and helped God's people.

5

Trouble in Israel

Joshua 7

DURING the battle of Jericho, a young man named Achan disobeyed God's command. He took some things from the city and hid them in his tent. He thought no one would find out, but God saw what Achan did, and he was very angry, because everything in Jericho belonged to him.

At first the Israelites didn't know anything was wrong, and Joshua went ahead with plans for the next battle.

He sent some men out to explore the land in the hills above Jericho. They walked up the road from Jericho into the hill country. On one of the hills they found a little city named Ai.

"It's a small city," they reported back to Joshua. "We need only two or three companies of men to conquer it. It's not necessary for all of us to go up there. Don't bother sending the whole army."

So three companies of Israelites marched up to the city of Ai. But as soon as they attacked, the men of Ai came out and chased them away. As the Israelites scrambled back down the slope to the Jordan Valley, the men of Ai killed about thirty-six of them.

They returned to the camp and told about the defeat. As the Israelites listened, they felt their courage melt away. Something was terribly wrong!

Joshua knew at once what the problem was. The Lord wasn't with them in the battle. He and the other leaders tore their clothes in grief and fell down on the ground in front of the ark. They lay there until evening with dust on their heads to show their sorrow.

"O Lord God," prayed Joshua, "why did you bring us across the Jordan, just to let our enemies defeat us? The Israelites have run away from the enemy, and I don't know why! The Canaanites will think they can beat us when they hear about this! They'll wipe us off the face of the earth!"

"Israel has sinned!" answered the Lord. "The

people have disobeyed me and have broken our covenant-agreement. Someone has taken what belongs to me. Someone has stolen from me, has lied about it, and has hidden my things among his own belongings! That's why I didn't help you at Ai, and that's why your enemies defeated you! Unless the Israelites bring back what was stolen, and punish the thief, they are condemned! I won't be with you anymore unless you do this!"

Then the Lord told Joshua how to find out who was guilty.

The next day Joshua called the people together and explained that they were in trouble because someone had stolen from the Lord. He called them forward, tribe by tribe, and the Lord showed him that the guilty person belonged to the tribe of Judah.

As everyone watched, Joshua called the tribe of Judah forward, clan by clan. The Lord picked out the clan of Zerah.

Then the clan of Zerah came forward, family by family. The guilty person belonged to the family of Zabdi.

Joshua called the family of Zabdi forward, person by person, and all Israel saw that the guilty one was Achan.

"My son," said Joshua, "honor the Lord and tell him the truth. Confess what you have done. Don't try to hide anything."

"I confess," said Achan. "I have sinned against the Lord! In Jericho I saw a beautiful Babylonian robe and some silver and a bar of gold. I wanted them so much, I took them. I buried them in the ground under my tent, with the silver at the bottom."

Joshua sent some men to Achan's tent, and they came back with the robe and the silver and the bar of gold.

Then he took Achan and the stolen things to a valley far out from the camp at Gigal. He took Achan's sons and daughters, his oxen and donkeys and sheep and goats, his tent and everything else that belonged to him. All the people of Israel went with them.

"Why have you brought this trouble to us?"

asked Joshua. "Now the Lord will bring trouble to you!"

Then the Israelites threw stones at Achan until he was dead. They burned all his belongings and piled a great heap of stones over the ashes.

From then on, that place was called Trouble Valley (Achor in Hebrew) because of the trouble that Achan brought to Israel.

6

Ambush at Ai

Joshua 8

AFTER the execution of Achan, the Lord wasn't angry with Israel anymore. He said to Joshua, "Take all your soldiers and march up to Ai. Don't be afraid. I'll conquer the king of Ai and his people and his city."

He told Joshua to set up an ambush to attack Ai by surprise.

Joshua chose some of his bravest soldiers and sent them out at night. "God is giving us victory over Ai," he said.

He told them what to do, and they went and

hid in a place west of Ai. Joshua and the others spent the night in the camp.

The next morning Joshua and the rest of his men marched up to Ai and camped on the north side of the city.

When the king of Ai found out that the Israelites were back, he hurried out with all his men to attack them. He had no idea that five more companies of Israelite soldiers were waiting in ambush west of the city.

Joshua and his men ran east, toward the wilderness, tricking the men of Ai into running after them. They lured them farther and farther away, leaving the city unguarded.

Then the Lord said to Joshua, "Point your spear at Ai. I'm going to conquer it for you."

As soon as Joshua lifted his spear, the Israelite soldiers hiding in ambush got up and ran into the city. They had no problem taking it, for not a single man was left behind to defend Ai. The Israelites captured the city and immediately set it on fire.

The men of Ai looked back and saw smoke rising from their city. Joshua and his men saw it, too, and they stopped running. They turned around and attacked. Then the Israelites inside the city joined the battle and surrounded the men of Ai. The Israelites cut them down with their swords, and none of them escaped.

Joshua kept pointing his spear at Ai until the battle was over. The Israelites killed twelve thou-

sand people that day—the whole population of the city of Ai. The Lord let them take some things for themselves, but everything else in the city was burned to the ground. Ai was in ruins forever.

After the battle Joshua led the people of Israel to a place in the hills between Mount Ebal and Mount Gerizim near the town of Shechem. Following directions given by Moses, he built an altar from great blocks of stone. He cut words into the stones, making a copy of the law of Moses. Then he offered sacrifices to the Lord on the altar.

Everyone listened as Joshua read God's teaching out loud. Men, women, and children heard how the Lord wanted them to love God and one another, to be kind and honest and never to worship idols.

Then Joshua told half the people to stand together, facing north, toward Mount Ebal. He read God's warnings to them.

If the Israelites disobeyed God's teaching, God would let their enemies defeat them, and he would drive them out of the Promised Land.

Then Joshua sent the other half of the people to stand at a place facing south, toward Mount Gerizim. He read God's blessings to them. If the Israelites obeyed God's teaching, God would give them everything they needed, and he would let them stay in the Promised Land forever.

After they heard God's teaching and the warnings and blessings, the people of Israel came down from the hills. They walked past the ruins of Ai, past the pile of stones at Achor, all the way back to the camp at Gilgal by the River Jordan.

7

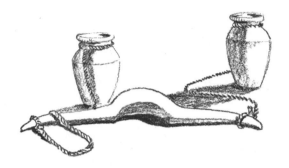

The Gibeonites Play a Trick on Joshua

Joshua 9

IN the hill country near Ai was a city called Gibeon. When the people of that city heard what Joshua had done to their neighbors, they decided not to fight but to try to save themselves by playing a trick on Joshua.

Some men from Gibeon put on old clothes and loaded their donkeys with worn-out saddlebags. Inside the bags they placed torn wineskins and moldy bread. Then they set out for the Israelite camp at Gilgal.

They arrived there in a few hours. They went

straight to Joshua and said, "We've come from a faraway land. We've heard of your great victories, and we're here to offer you our friendship. Will you make a peace treaty with us?"

"Who are you and where do you come from?" asked Joshua.

"As we said, sir, from a faraway land. We've heard about the Lord, your God, and what he did in Egypt and how he defeats everyone who fights against you."

"Perhaps you live near here," said Joshua. "If you do, we can't make a treaty with you."

"But look," said the Gibeonites. "See our bread. We took it hot from the oven, and now it's dry and moldy. These wineskins were brand-new when we filled them. Now look! They're all split. You can see for yourself how old and ragged our clothes and sandals are. They're worn out from the long journey!"

Without asking the Lord what to do, the leaders of Israel made a peace treaty with the men of Gibeon.

Three days later some of the Israelites went to investigate, and they found that Gibeon was nearby. They had been tricked!

They came back to the camp very angry. They wanted to kill the Gibeonites. But the Israelite leaders said, "You know we made a treaty in the name of the Lord. If we break our promise, we'll bring trouble to Israel. We can't kill the Gibeonites, but we can punish them. Let's make

them our servants. We can give them the worst jobs to do. We'll make them cut our wood and carry our water. God won't punish us for that."

The Israelites agreed to this plan, and Joshua sent a message to the Gibeonites.

They answered, "We tricked you because we found out that the Lord, your God, ordered Moses to take this whole country and to kill everyone who lives here. We were terrified of you! But we're in your power now. Do whatever you think is right."

So Joshua protected the Gibeonites from the anger of the Israelites, and from that day on, they cut wood and carried water for Israel.

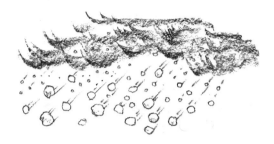

Conquering the Land

Joshua 10—12

ALL over Canaan the people were talking about the Israelite victories at Jericho and Ai. In the hill country, in the lowlands, and on the seacoast the news spread. The kings of the Canaanite city-states began to make plans for war.

When Adoni-zedek, king of Jerusalem, heard that the Gibeonites had made peace with the Israelites, he was very upset. Gibeon was a large, important city just north of Jerusalem, and its men were brave fighters.

Adoni-zedek sent a message to the kings of four cities south of Jerusalem. "Come, help me attack Gibeon!" he said. "Let's join forces to punish them, for they've made a treaty with our enemy!"

All five kings brought armies to Gibeon, and they surrounded the city.

The Gibeonites sent an urgent message to Joshua at Gilgal. "Come quickly and help us! All the kings of the hill country have come together to attack us!"

According to the treaty, the Israelites were supposed to protect the Gibeonites.

Joshua was worried. How could he fight five armies?

Then the Lord said to Joshua, "Don't be afraid I'll defeat those kings. None of them will be able to do a thing to you!"

Joshua left immediately with his men, marching all night on the uphill road from Gilgal to Gibeon. He would surprise the armies of the five kings by sneaking up on them in the darkness.

The Lord made the Canaanites panic when they saw the Israelites, and they fled in terror. Joshua's men chased them westward away from Gibeon, down through the passes between the hills. The Canaanites ran as fast as they could, and as they ran, the Lord threw huge hailstones at them. More were killed by the hailstones than by Israelite swords!

An old book called the book of Jasher includes

a song about this battle. In the song, Joshua prays before the battle, and the Lord answers with a miracle.

> O sun, stand still over Gibeon,
> And moon, stop over the valley of Aijalon!
>
> The sun stood still, and the moon didn't move until the Israelites defeated their enemies.

The five kings escaped from Gibeon and went to hide in a nearby cave. Joshua sent some men to roll large stones in front of the cave. "Place guards there," he ordered, "and the rest of you

chase after anyone else who has escaped. Don't let anyone get back to the safety of those walled cities! The Lord your God has defeated the enemy. Now go get them!"

The Israelite soldiers did as Joshua ordered, and they captured most of those who survived the battle. Only a few Canaanites made it safely home.

When Joshua met his men at the cave, he told them, "Open the entrance of the cave and bring out those kings!"

They rolled away the stones and brought out the five Canaanite kings. Then Joshua called his men together and ordered the officers to put their feet on the necks of the kings.

"Don't be afraid!" said Joshua. "Be brave! Just look—this is what the Lord will do to all your enemies!"

Then Joshua killed the five kings and the soldiers threw the bodies into the cave. They sealed the entrance back up with rocks.

Next Joshua led his men to the cities of the five kings. After a long war they conquered the cities because the Lord God fought for Israel.

News of the Israelite victories in the south spread far and wide. In the north of Canaan, King Jabin of Hazor heard what had happened, and he sent messages to other kings of the north. They gathered a great army and pitched camp together at the Waters of Merom, near Lake Huleh, ready to fight the Israelites. They had more soldiers and horses and chariots than anyone could count.

When the Israelites heard about the great army gathering in the north, they were terrified, for they had only foot soldiers. How could the Israelites possibly win?

"Don't be afraid," the Lord said to Joshua. "By this time tomorrow, I'll conquer that enormous army. Just follow my instructions."

Joshua and his soldiers marched north from Gilgal. When they arrived at the Waters of Merom, they sneaked up on the enemy. They crippled their horses and burned their chariots, as the Lord directed them. The Lord gave them victory, and they chased the Canaanites as far as Sidon, a seaport in the far north.

Then Joshua and his men battled the cities of the kings who had fought against them. Like the war in the south, this northern war took many years. When it was over, the Israelites were in control of a large part of the land of Canaan.

Joshua led the Israelite army in the land west of the Jordan River, as Moses had led them in the land east of the Jordan. But in all the battles, east and west, the Lord won the victory. The war against the Canaanites was the Lord's war. It was his power that defeated the enemy. He wanted to drive the Canaanites out because they worshiped idols and did evil deeds. He used the Israelites to show his great power to the nations of the world.

9

Dividing the Land

Joshua 13—19, 21

AFTER the long war to conquer Canaan, the Lord said to Joshua, "You're getting very old. I want you to divide the Promised Land among the Israelites before you die. It's time for the Israelites to settle in the land I'm giving to them."

Then the leaders of the tribe of Judah brought an old man to see Joshua. He was Caleb, a warrior from the old days.

"Remember what the Lord told Moses," Caleb told Joshua. "When I was forty years old, Moses sent you and me out to spy on this land. Twelve spies went out, but only you and I brought back honest reports. The other spies frightened the people. They said the land was poor and the Canaanites were powerful. The Israelites didn't believe that the Lord could give us this land. Because they didn't trust the Lord, he made us wait forty years in the wilderness. But I obeyed the Lord, and Moses promised me I could have whatever part of the land I wanted. Well, look at me! I'm eighty-five years old now, and just as strong as ever! Let me have the hill country around the city of Hebron. That's where we saw those giant people called Anaks, living in great walled cities. With the Lord's help, I'll drive them out!"

Joshua blessed his old friend Caleb and gave him the land he requested.

Then he divided the rest of the land according to directions that the Lord had given to Moses. Joshua gave land by tribes to all the people, not just the leaders, so each Israelite family owned some land. He divided it fairly, with the larger tribes getting more land, and the smaller tribes less.

The tribes of Reuben and Gad and half the tribe of Manasseh already had received land from Moses on the east side of the Jordan River.

On the west side of the river, the first tribe to settle was the tribe of Judah. Judah took the southern hill country. The smaller tribes of Simeon and Benjamin settled beside them.

Next the tribe of Ephraim and the other half of the tribe of Manasseh took the land in the central hill country.

Ephraim was the largest and most powerful of all the tribes. Joshua was a member of that tribe, and he received some land in that territory.

In the northern part of Canaan, Joshua gave land to the tribes of Zebulun, Issachar, Asher, and Naphtali.

The tribe of Dan settled between the southern hills and the seacoast. Many years later they were forced out by the people who lived there, and they moved to the far north.

The Kenites, a desert tribe related to the family of Moses' wife, settled in the wilderness south of Judah. They had traveled all the way

from Midian to Canaan with the Israelites, and now they settled among them.

The tribe of Levi received no land, because the men of that tribe were set apart from the other Israelites to serve as priests for the whole nation. The Levite priests led worship services and taught the people the laws of God.

After Joshua divided the land, the leaders of the tribe of Levi said to Eleazar, the high priest, "The Lord told Moses to give us cities to live in and pastureland for our cattle."

So Eleazar and Joshua gave the Levites some cities in the territory of all the other tribes. The Levites had no land of their own, but they were scattered in the land of all the other tribes. This way, they could live among all the people and teach them God's ways.

Each of these groups of tribes—in the east beyond the Jordan, in the central hill country, in the southern hill country, and in the far north—was separated from all the others by rivers and mountains and valleys, and by the Canaanite cities which lay between them.

At this time the Israelites didn't settle in the lowlands and along the seacoast, for the Lord had not driven out all the Canaanites. The Canaanites still lived in those areas and in the valley of Jezreel between the northern tribes and the hill country.

The Lord told Joshua that if the Israelites obeyed him, some day he would force out the rest of the Canaanites, even the most powerful ones.

But for now the Israelites settled down near the Canaanite temples, altars, and idols. They moved away from the camp at Gilgal and into the land which the Lord had given them.

At a place called Shiloh, in the central hill country, they set up God's tabernacle as a place of worship for all the tribes, and inside the tabernacle they placed the ark. In front of the tabernacle Joshua set up the great altar and the Levite priests offered sacrifices to thank God for giving them the land.

10

Cities of Refuge

Joshua 20—21

AFTER Joshua divided the land among the tribes of Israel, the Lord gave him some special instructions.

According to an ancient custom, if a person killed someone, it was the duty of the nearest relative of the dead person to take the life of the killer. He did this whether the killing was an accident or a planned murder. The nearest relative, who was called the "avenger " or "redeemer of blood," went looking for the killer, to get even.

God had given a new law to Moses. According

to this teaching, if someone killed a person by accident, he could find safety from the avenger in a "city of refuge." If he could get to the city before the avenger caught him, the leaders of the city took him in, listened to his story, and gave him a home. The people of the city would not turn him over to the avenger. He could stay in the city until he received a fair trial, or until the high priest died and another high priest took his place. Then he could safely return to his own home.

The Lord told Joshua to set aside six towns as cities of refuge, three on the east side of the Jordan, and three on the west side. There would be a city of refuge in every part of the land.

This law helped end a terrible custom called blood feuding, in which people took revenge even if an injury was done by accident. It was one of

the many ways God was teaching his people how to live.

When the long war was over and the people were settled in the land, the Israelites realized that the Lord had kept all his promises. He had led them to the Promised Land, he had defeated their enemies, and he had given them homes of their own. Now he gave them peace in the land.

11

The Witness by the River

Joshua 22

AS the tribes of Israel packed up their tents and prepared to move to their new homes, Joshua called together the men of Reuben and Gad and East Manasseh.

"You've done everything that Moses told you to do, and you've obeyed all my orders," he said. "It's been a long war, and you've never deserted us. From beginning to end, you've faithfully obeyed the Lord your God. Now the Lord has given us peace, as he promised. It's time for you to go back to your land on the other side of the

Jordan. When you get there, be sure to obey God's instructions. Love the Lord and serve him with all your heart and mind."

Then Joshua blessed them and sent them home.

They took with them many cattle, a lot of silver and gold, bronze and iron items, and clothing, all the things they had captured from their enemies.

At the banks of the Jordan River, the men of Reuben and Gad and East Manasseh stopped. They took some rocks and piled them up. Then they continued on their way home.

The other Israelites heard rumors about the rocks by the river. They were annoyed and angry.

"God commanded one altar for all the tribes!" they said. "Those eastern tribes have gone and built an altar on our side of the Jordan, when we already have an altar at Shiloh!"

They talked about going to war. But first they sent Phinehas, son of Eleazar, the high priest, to investigate. The leaders of Israel went with him.

"We have a message for you," they said when they came to Gilead, the land in the east. "Why have you done this awful thing against the God of Israel? Building your own altar is turning away from the Lord! Remember what happened when Achan disobeyed God at Jericho! Don't bring trouble to Israel!"

"The Lord is the Mighty One, the God of gods!" answered the people of the eastern tribes. "He

knows why we built this. It's a monument to remind us that we belong to him. We aren't rebelling!"

Then they explained why they built the monument.

"We were worried," they said. "We thought that some day your children would tell our children they don't belong to the Lord because they live over here in the east. We were afraid our children would stop worshiping the Lord! So we built this as a sign for those who come after us, for our descendants and yours, to show them that we do worship the Lord! We'll join you on your side of the Jordan on holy days. This is a monument, not an altar for worship!"

"We believe you," said Phinehas, "and now we

know that the Lord is with us. No one has sinned, and God won't be angry with Israel."

Then Phinehas and the leaders of Israel went back to the land of Canaan. They were satisfied. They reported the news to the others, and they were satisfied, too. The people of the western tribes praised God and stopped talking about going to war.

The people of the eastern tribes said, "This is a witness between us that the Lord is truly God!"

12

Choosing the Lord

Joshua 23—24

ONE day many years after the Israelites first entered the Promised Land, Joshua called the people together to give them his last words. He was an old, old man now and he wanted to talk to them one more time before he died.

They met at Shechem, in the middle of the land, near Joshua's home. This was near the place they had heard God's teachings and warnings and blessings when they first came into the land. It was also the place their ancestor Abraham first received God's promise of the land.

Joshua brought the Israelites a message from the Lord. He began by telling them the story of God and his people.

"Long ago," he said, "your ancestors lived far away, on the other side of the Euphrates River. They didn't know the Lord. They worshiped idols. Then the Lord called Abraham to leave his home and come to the land of Canaan. He made Abraham the father of a special family, a family who would grow into a great nation and be a blessing to all nations of the earth.

"The Lord gave him a son, Isaac, and Isaac had two sons, Jacob and Esau. The Lord gave Esau the hill country of Edom, but Jacob and his children went down to Egypt.

"Jacob's family grew into a nation of many people. For four hundred years they suffered as slaves in Egypt, and then the Lord rescued them. He sent his servant, Moses, to lead his people out of slavery, and he struck the Egyptians with terrible punishments.

"When the Egyptians on their horses and chariots chased after the Israelites, the Israelites cried out to the Lord and he dried up the sea so his people could escape. Then he made the sea flow back over the Egyptians and drown them.

"The Lord chose the Israelites to be his people, and he made a special agreement with them called the covenant.

"Your parents wandered in the wilderness for forty years while the Lord tested them and taught them how to live. Finally, he brought you into this land.

"He spread panic before you, to drive out the Canaanites. *It was the Lord, not your swords and bows that defeated your enemies!*

"The Lord let you settle here in homes of your own. He gave you land which you didn't clear and cities which you didn't build. You eat from vineyards and olive groves which you didn't plant. The Lord your God gave you everything he promised.

"Now you must keep your part of the agreement. Honor the Lord and serve him. Get rid of the gods your ancestors worshiped, and worship only the Lord. If you don't want to serve the Lord, decide today whom you will serve— either the gods of your ancestors or the gods of the Canaanites.

"As for me and my family, we will serve the Lord!"

The people listened carefully to Joshua. They answered him, saying, "We'll never leave the Lord to worship other gods! The Lord our God brought us out of slavery. He took care of us in the wilderness. He drove out our enemies and gave us this land. We will serve the Lord, for he is our God!"

"Remember," warned Joshua, "you can't serve the Lord and other gods at the same time. If you leave him to worship any other gods, he'll punish you!"

"We want to serve the Lord!" they answered.

"Then throw away your foreign gods and turn with all your heart to the Lord," Joshua said. "Obey him."

"We will serve the Lord! We promise," said the people again.

Then Joshua wrote down the covenant, so the people would remember their agreement with the Lord. He put a large stone in place under a great oak tree.

"This stone will be our witness," he said. "You have promised to love and obey the Lord. You know in your hearts that he always keeps his promises. The rest is up to you!"

Then the people went back to their homes in

the different parts of the land. Soon afterward, Joshua died. He was one hundred and ten years old.

After they buried Joshua in his land in the hills of Ephraim, the Israelites buried the body of their ancestor, Joseph. They had brought Joseph's body in a stone coffin all the way from Egypt. Now they put it in land which Joseph's father, Jacob, had purchased many years before at Shechem.

As long as Joshua was alive, the Israelites obeyed the Lord. Joshua's name means "the Lord will save," or "savior." He was a great savior of Israel.

The people of Israel kept on obeying the Lord after Joshua died. They obeyed the Lord as long as the leaders who served with Joshua were living. As long as they obeyed the Lord, they enjoyed peace in the land.

Judges Save the People

13

God Warns the Weepers

Judges 1—3

THE Israelites were the only people in the world who worshiped the Lord. Everyone else bowed down to idols. The Canaanites worshiped many different gods, but Baal, the god of storm and rain, and Asherah, the goddess of love and war, were their favorites. Altars to Baal and poles carved in the image of Asherah stood all over the land of Canaan. The Canaanite farmers prayed to these idols and offered them sacrifices. They hoped that these gods would give them healthy herds, good crops, and many children.

When the Israelites settled in the land of Canaan, they built houses and planted crops, and took care of their herds and families. They began to follow many of the customs of the people living near them.

Gradually, everyone who had seen all the great things that the Lord had done for them died, and the people who came after them forgot the Lord. They began to act like the Canaanites, and soon they were bowing down to idols. They disobeyed God's instructions and stopped worshiping the Lord. Instead, they worshiped images of wood and stone. They offered sacrifices to the idols and prayed to them as their Canaanite neighbors did.

The Lord was angry with the Israelites. When they began to do evil like the people all around them, he punished them. He let raiders bother them and robbers overpower them.

Then one day the Lord sent an angel to warn the people. The angel brought this message from God: "I brought you out of Egypt and into this land which I promised to your ancestors. I promised them I wouldn't be the one to break the covenant I made with them. But you have disobeyed me! You haven't kept your part of the agreement.

"Listen to me," continued the angel of the Lord. "You must stay away from the Canaanites. Don't make agreements with them. Don't marry them or copy their bad behavior. Destroy their altars. Watch out, or their gods will trap you!"

When the Israelites heard these words, they began to cry. They prayed to the Lord and offered sacrifices to him. Because of this, the place where the angel appeared was called Bochim, which means "weepers."

The Lord heard the prayers of his people and sent help. But when the danger was past, the Israelites forgot the Lord and started to worship other gods again. This went on for several hundred years. The people would sin, the Lord would punish them, they would cry out, and he would help them. Each generation was worse than the one before. Almost no one in Israel remembered the Lord.

"The Israelites are breaking the covenant!" the Lord said. "If they won't serve me, I won't destroy their enemies! I'll let their enemies stay

here in the land and I'll use them to test the Israelites!"

As the people's behavior became worse and worse, the Lord allowed their enemies to become crueler and crueler to them. The enemy rulers forced the Israelites to bring the best part of their crops as a kind of tax.

The Israelites began by serving idols, and they ended by serving foreign rulers. Worst of all, they fought among themselves.

But God didn't give up on his people. Each time the Israelites turned back to the Lord their God, he sent someone to save them from their enemies. These leaders were called judges.

Over a period of several hundred years there were twelve judges, one from each of the twelve tribes of Israel. But even the judges sometimes disobeyed God's teaching and did cruel and wicked things.

These were the days when most people in Israel forgot that the Lord was their King. Instead of obeying the Lord, they did whatever they pleased.

14

The Message in the Hidden Sword

Judges 3

THE first foreign ruler who conquered the Israelites was Cushan Risha-thaim. He oppressed them cruelly for eight years. The Lord allowed this to happen because the Israelites were sinning against him and worshiping Baal and Asherah.

Then the Israelites cried out to the Lord, and he sent someone to save them. This was Othniel, a nephew of the old warrior, Caleb. Othniel was the first judge in Israel.

The spirit of the Lord came over Othniel and he

led the men of his tribe, Judah, against Cushan. The Lord gave them victory and the land was at peace for forty years.

But after Othniel died, the Israelites again did evil things, and again the Lord punished them.

This time the Lord gave strength to Eglon, king of Moab. Eglon raised a great army and invaded the hill country of central Canaan. He attacked and conquered the tribe of Benjamin and ruled over them for eighteen years.

Then the people cried out to the Lord for mercy, and he answered their prayers. He sent another judge to set them free, a left-handed man from the tribe of Benjamin named Ehud.

One day Ehud made himself a short sword with two sharp edges. He knew that nobody would look for a weapon on his right side, so he hid it under his clothes on his right side. Most people were right-handed and wore weapons on their left sides.

Ehud went with the men who took gifts as tribute to King Eglon. They delivered these taxes to Eglon's palace at the palm trees near Jericho, and when they left, Ehud went with them. He walked as far as the carved stones near Gilgal, and then he turned back toward the palace.

When he arrived, the guards recognized him from his earlier visit. He seemed harmless. They saw that he had no weapon on his left side, so they let him in to see the king.

Some servants took Ehud up to the room on

the palace roof where King Eglon was cooling off. It was a hot day, and Eglon was a very fat man.

Ehud glanced around the room. "I have a private message for you, O king!" he said.

Eglon ordered his servants to leave the room.

Then Ehud went up to the king and said, "I have a secret message for you from God!"

King Eglon stood up.

Ehud reached for his sword with his left hand. He pulled it from under his cloak and plunged it into King Eglon's enormous stomach.

Ehud had accomplished his mission. Knowing that the king was dying, Ehud closed the doors and escaped over the balcony.

A few minutes later Eglon's servants came to the door. It was locked.

71

"He just wants some privacy," one of them said.

After a while they began to argue about what to do. They were beginning to think that something was the matter. Then one of the servants found a key and unlocked the door.

Inside they found their master lying on the floor, dead! The Moabites were helpless without their king. They panicked and began to flee towards Moab.

Meanwhile Ehud had reached the hill country of Ephraim. He blew a trumpet to call the Israelites to battle.

"Follow me!" he shouted, and he led them down from the hills. They found the Moabites already running away in terror.

"The Lord has given us victory over the Moabites!" shouted Ehud, and led the Israelites to the Jordan River.

When the Moabites reached the river, they found Ehud and his men waiting for them. The Israelites blocked all the shallow places of the Jordan so the Moabites couldn't get across. They easily defeated them, killing ten whole companies of Moabites.

Ehud was judge in Israel until he died, and there was peace in the land for eighty years.

Then the Philistines began to bother the Israelites. The Philistines were people from the islands of the Aegean Sea, near Greece. They had entered the land of Canaan about the same time as the Israelites. They took over the seacoast of southern Canaan and towns and villages near Dan and Judah. They had five great cities, each with its own king.

Then the Lord sent a man named Shamgar to be a judge in Israel. Shamgar led the Israelites in driving back the Philistines with oxgoads. These were the long poles with metal spikes which farmers used to control their oxen. With them, Shamgar killed six hundred Philistines.

15

The Song of Deborah

Judges 4—5

WHEN the Israelites began to worship idols again, the Lord let Jabin, a king in northern Canaan, conquer them. Jabin cruelly oppressed the Israelites in the territory of Naphtali and Zebulun for twenty years. They had to bring so many tax gifts to Jabin that they didn't have enough to eat.

The Israelites were afraid of Jabin because Sisera, the captain of Jabin's army, had nine hundred iron-plated chariots and many soldiers with iron weapons.

The Canaanites, like the Philistines, knew the secret of making tools and weapons from iron ore. In those days most people, including the Israelites, knew how to melt copper and tin together to make bronze, but they didn't know how to make iron from iron ore. Since iron was much stronger than bronze, the Israelites were weak and afraid.

Then the Lord sent Deborah, a prophet who judged Israel. People came to her from all over the land for advice. Deborah sat under a palm tree at a place near Bethel in the central hill country and told the people the will of God.

She knew what cruel things Jabin and Sisera were doing, so she sent a message to a brave Israelite soldier who lived in Naphtali. His name was Barak.

"Here's an order for you from the Lord, the God of Israel," Deborah told Barak. "Gather an army from the northern tribes and lead them to Mount Tabor, at the edge of the Valley of Jezreel. The Lord will bring Sisera and his soldiers to meet you at the Kishon River. Sisera will have nine hundred iron chariots, but the Lord will give you the victory!"

Barak answered, "I'll go if you go with me, but if you don't go with me, I won't go!"

"All right," said Deborah, "I'll go with you. But you won't get any glory for this victory, because the Lord will defeat Sisera through the power of a woman!"

Then Deborah rose from her seat under the palm tree and went to meet Barak at Kadesh in Naphtali. Barak followed her advice and called out the men from the tribes of Naphtali and Zebulun. Ten companies of farmers with crude bronze weapons followed Barak to Mount Tabor at the edge of the valley of Jezreel.

When Sisera heard that the Israelites were camped at Mount Tabor, he brought his whole army of professional soldiers with iron weapons and chariots to the banks of the Kishon River.

The Kishon River ran through the Valley of Jezreel, but when the Canaanite army arrived, the riverbed was dry. They rode their horses and chariots right through the dust in the middle of it.

From the top of Mount Tabor the Israelites looked down and saw Sisera's army. It looked unbeatable.

"Go on!" cried Deborah. "Now is the time! The Lord is giving you the victory today! He'll march in front of you!"

Barak and his men overcame their fear and went charging down the side of the mountain.

Sisera's army was taken by surprise. While they were wondering what to do about the Israelite charge, the Lord sent a great thunderstorm. Heavy rain poured down, turning the dry ground into mud and swelling the little stream into a mighty, rushing river! The water came foaming and roaring over the Canaanites, sweeping the soldiers away!

The horses stamped the ground with their hoofs, but they couldn't pull the chariot wheels out of the mud.

Sisera himself was so frightened that he jumped down from his chariot and ran out of the valley on foot. His soldiers tried to run up the valley toward the mountain, but they were trapped by the flood. Sisera ran in the opposite direction.

While Barak's men chased Sisera's soldiers, Sisera escaped. He found a tent standing alone at the edge of the valley and he ran there for shelter.

In front of the tent stood Jael, the wife of Heber, a Kenite. The Kenites were friends of the Israelites, but Sisera thought the tent of this desert family would be a safe place to hide.

Jael recognized the great Canaanite warrior. "Come in, sir. Come into my tent. Don't be afraid."

He went into her tent, and she covered him with a rug.

"I'm thirsty," he said. "Please give me some water."

Jael opened a leather bag of goat's milk. She poured some into a large bowl and gave it to Sisera. Then she covered him again with the rug.

"Stand over there, at the entrance of the tent," said Sisera as he drank the milk. "If anyone comes and asks if somebody's here, say no."

He was so tired from the battle and from running that he fell sound asleep.

As Sisera slept, Jael reached with her left hand for a wooden peg, the kind that fastened tent ropes to the ground. With her right hand she took the wooden mallet for hammering in the pegs.

She crept softly up behind Sisera. As he lay sleeping, she hammered the peg through his head and killed him.

Jael looked out of the tent and saw Barak coming toward her.

She went out to meet him.

"In here!" she called. "I'll show you the man you're looking for!"

Barak followed Jael into the tent, and there was the man he was chasing. There was Sisera on the ground, dead, with the tent peg through his skull!

Back at Sisera's home, the Canaanite women were lounging, waiting for the soldiers to return.

Sisera's mother leaned out the window, watching for him. "Why is his chariot so late?" she asked. "Why are the horses so slow?"

One of her maids answered, "They've stopped to steal some presents for us! An embroidered scarf for me! Two scarves for the head of Sisera!"

At Kadesh, Deborah and Barak were singing a victory song. "Praise the Lord!" they sang,

> For he has won the victory!
> And blessed be Jael,
>   who has killed the enemy!
> O Lord, may all your enemies die like that one!
> And may all your friends shine like the rising sun!

They kept on singing about the battle. All over Israel people gathered to play instruments and sing the "Song of Deborah." Rich people and poor people met together at the town wells to hear how the Lord had humiliated Sisera and defeated his chariots.

After this, the land was at peace for forty years.

16

Gideon Cuts Down an Altar

Judges 6

WHEN the Israelites began sinning and worshiping idols again, the Lord punished them by letting the Midianites rule over them.

The Midianites were tribesmen from the eastern desert who came into the land of Canaan at harvesttime to steal the Israelites' grain. They rode in on their camels, traveling much faster than the Israelites on their donkeys.

These raiders bothered the Israelites for seven years. Each time the Israelites were ready to harvest their crops, the Midianites came and camped on their land and attacked them. The Midianites raided the Israelites' land as far west as Gaza, taking everything they could carry away with them. They left nothing behind for the Israelites to eat, not even food for their animals.

The Midianites seemed as thick as grasshoppers, bringing their own cattle and setting up their own tents. There were more of them than anyone could count. After they stole the crops, their animals ate the grass!

The Israelites were helpless. All they could do was hide from the raiders in caves in the hills. They put grain in secret places so they wouldn't starve.

They were suffering so much that finally they cried out to the Lord for help. He answered them by sending another judge to rescue them.

A man named Gideon was pounding out some wheat one day in a hidden place near his home in the town of Ophrah in the territory of West Manasseh. He was beating the wheat with a stick in the bottom of the grape press, where wine was made. This was harder and slower work than using the threshing floor, but the Midianites couldn't see him in the grape press.

Suddenly Gideon saw a stranger sitting under an oak tree nearby.

"The Lord is with you, mighty warrior!" said the stranger.

"Oh sir," answered Gideon, "if the Lord is with us, then why have all these terrible things been happening? Where are the miracles we've heard about? The Lord rescued us from the Egyptians and all our other enemies, but where is he now? I think the Lord has gone away and left us to the Midianites! They have us in the palms of their hands!"

"You can save Israel," said the stranger. "I will give you the strength to rescue Israel from the power of the Midianites!"

Was the stranger bringing him a message from the Lord?

"Oh, sir," said Gideon, "how can I save Israel? My family is the least important in the tribe of Manasseh, and I am the least important in my family!"

"I am sending you!" answered the stranger. "You will crush the Midianites as easily as if they were one man!"

"Sir," said Gideon, "if this is really a message from the Lord, give me a sign. Don't go away. I'll be right back."

"I'm not going anywhere," said the stranger.

Gideon went into his house and cooked a young goat and baked some flat bread. He put the meat in a basket and the broth in a pot. Then he brought the food out to the stranger, who was waiting in the shade of the oak tree.

Gideon gave him the gifts, but the stranger would not eat.

"Take the meat and the bread and put them on that rock," he said. "Pour the broth over them."

Gideon did as he was told.

Then the stranger reached out and touched the meat and bread with the tip of the rod he was carrying in his hand.

Fire burst out of the rock and burned up the food! While it was burning, the stranger disappeared right in front of Gideon's eyes!

Gideon realized that the stranger was the angel of the Lord. He cried out, in terror, "O Lord God! I have seen your messenger face to face!" Could a man see an angel of God and still live?

"Peace be with you," said the Lord. "Don't be afraid. You won't die."

Gideon built an altar under the oak tree and called it "The Lord Is Peace."

That night the Lord spoke to Gideon in a

dream, telling him how to end the Israelites' idol worship. This was necessary before he could set them free from the Midianites.

While it was still dark, Gideon rose and went out with ten of his servants and cut down his father's altar to Baal. They also cut down the sacred pole of Asherah which stood next to it. In its place they built an altar to the Lord. Gideon took his father's prize bull and burned it on the altar as a sacrifice to the Lord. He used the idol for firewood!

The next morning the people of Ophrah found that the altar of Baal was gone, and so was the pole of Asherah. There, on the exact spot where the idols had stood, was an altar to the Lord! And there on the altar was Joash's bull, all burnt up!

"Who did this?" they asked each other.

Someone answered, "Gideon did it!"

"Bring your son out to us!" said the men of Ophrah to Joash. "We'll kill him for this!"

"Are you defending your god?" asked Joash, the father of Gideon. "Does he need you to rescue him? If Baal is really a god, he can take care of himself! It was his altar that was torn down—let Baal defend himself!"

When the people realized that Baal could do nothing, they began to worship the Lord.

Gideon was living up to his name, which means "hacker," or "one who cuts down." After this day, he was also known as Jerubbaal, which means "Let Baal defend himself."

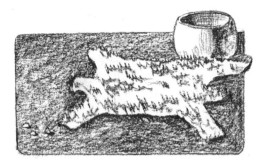

17

The Little Army That Won a Great Victory

Judges 6—7

THE enemies of Israel were gathering their forces. The combined armies of the Midianites and other desert tribes from the east crossed the Jordan River and camped in the Valley of Jezreel, ready to attack.

The spirit of the Lord came over Gideon, and he blew a trumpet to call the people to follow him. He sent messengers all through the territory of Manasseh, and the men from his tribe came to join him. Next he sent word to the tribes of Asher, Zebulun, and Naphtali, and they prepared to join the battle.

Gideon prayed to the Lord before he gave orders to his army.

"You said you'd save Israel through me," he said. "Please give me another sign, so I can be sure. I'll spread a fleece of wool on the threshing floor. Tomorrow morning, if there's dew on the wool and not on the ground, I'll know that you'll rescue Israel through me."

Gideon got up the next morning and found the wool so wet he was able to fill a bowl with the water he squeezed out of it. And the ground around the wool was dry!

"Please don't be angry," Gideon prayed, "but let me ask you just one more thing. Let me have another sign. Tomorrow morning let the wool be dry and the ground around it wet with dew."

The next morning Gideon found the wool dry and the ground all around it wet with dew!

Now he was sure that the Lord was with him and his army. He took his men and camped on the side of Mount Gilboa. The Midianites were camped in the valley below.

"Your army is too large," the Lord said to Gideon. "If I give the Israelites victory with an army this big, they'll think they did it all by themselves! They'll be sure their own power saved them. Tell your men that anyone who is frightened must go home."

Gideon gave his men the message, and twenty-two companies of soldiers went home. Ten com-

panies stayed, numbering several thousand men.

"You still have too many soldiers," said the Lord. "Take them down to the water, and I'll test them. I'll tell you which ones to take with you and which ones to send home."

Gideon took the soldiers down to the water and told them to drink. On one side he put all the men who lapped up the water with their tongues, like dogs. On the other side he put all those who kneeled down to drink, scooping up the water with their hands. Only three hundred lapped with their tongues. All the others kneeled down to drink.

"I'll save Israel with these three hundred men,"

said the Lord. "Send the others home."

Gideon and the three hundred men watched while all the other soldiers left. The little army looked down into the valley at the Midianites. There were thousands of them!

That night the Lord spoke to Gideon again. "Get up!" he said. "Attack the Midianites tonight, while it's still dark. I'll defeat them! I know you're afraid, so listen carefully. Sneak down to the Midianite camp right now with your servant, Purah. When you hear what the Midianites are saying about you, you'll have the courage you need!"

Gideon and Purah crept down in the darkness to the edge of the enemy camp. The tents of the Midianites were spread out along the valley as thick as a swarm of grasshoppers, and there were more camels than anyone could count.

When they arrived, two guards happened to be talking.

"I just had a dream," one of them said. "I dreamed that a stale loaf of barley bread came rolling into our camp. It hit one of the tents so hard that the tent collapsed!"

The other guard understood the meaning of the dream. "The barley loaf is the farmers of Israel, and the tent is the people of the desert," he explained. "The Israelite farmers will come into our camp and our army will collapse! God has given them victory over Midian, and our whole army is in their power!"

When Gideon heard this, he bowed down to worship the Lord. Then he and Purah went back to their camp. He had the courage he needed.

"Get up!" Gideon shouted to his men. "The Lord has put the Midianites into our power!"

He passed out a trumpet, a jar, and a torch to each of his men.

"Watch me," he said. "When we get down to the edge of the Midianite camp, do just as I do!"

They sneaked down in the darkness, holding the trumpets in their right hands and the jars in their left hands, with the torches hidden inside the clay jars.

Gideon divided them into three groups and told them to surround the enemy camp.

When Gideon gave the signal, each man blew his trumpet and smashed his jar. From every direction came the sound of trumpets and crashing jars and the flashing light of the torches.

"For the Lord and for Gideon!" they all shouted at once.

The Midianites woke from their sleep. What was the fierce noise all around them? Where were all those lights coming from? They were surrounded! It looked and sounded like an enormous army!

They jumped out of bed, shouting, and in the darkness they tripped and stumbled over each other. As they tried to escape, they swung their swords at each other. The Midianites were so confused and terrified that many of them killed each other in the darkness.

The rest of them ran away, trying to escape across the Jordan and back home to Midian.

Gideon's Revenge

Judges 7—8

THE Midianites were headed for the Jordan River. Their kings, Zebah and Zalmunna, made it safely across, and many others were following them.

Gideon sent a message to the Israelites who were sent home before the battle. He wanted them to come back and help him catch the Midianites who were running away.

He sent other messengers into the hills of Ephraim, asking the Ephraimites to join him.

"Capture the crossing places of the Jordan

River!" he told them. "Don't let the Midianites get away!"

The Ephraimites went to the shallow places of the Jordan and caught the two Midianite commanders, Oreb and Zeeb. Then they went to Gideon to complain.

"Why didn't you ask us to come earlier?" they asked. "You fought the battle without us!"

"That was nothing!" said Gideon. "The battle was easy compared to what you just did! Your cleanup work is much more important. God put Oreb and Zeeb into your power and you captured them!"

When they heard these peaceful words, the Ephraimites felt better, and they weren't angry anymore.

Then Gideon and his men crossed the Jordan River. By the time they arrived at the town of Succoth in Gilead they were exhausted and very hungry.

"Please give my men a few loaves of bread," Gideon said to the leaders of the town. "They're worn out from chasing the Midianites. We caught the commanders, and we still hope to get the kings, Zebah and Zalmunna."

"Why should we help you?" asked the leaders of Succoth. "You haven't captured those kings, and maybe you never will! Why should we feed your soldiers and make the Midianites mad at us?"

"If that's all you have to say, then watch out!"

warned Gideon. "When the Lord hands Zebah and Zalmunna over to me, I'll come back here and beat you with desert thorns and briars!"

Gideon and his men left Succoth and went to Penuel. He asked the people there the same thing, and they gave him the same answer.

"I'll come back!" he warned, "and when I do, I'll tear down the tower of Penuel!"

Then Gideon and his men went on their way. They followed the caravan road along the edge of the desert until they reached the place where the Midianites were camped. Only fifteen companies of them were left. The Israelites had killed a hundred and twenty companies of them in the battle.

Gideon and his men surprised the Midianites

and captured Zebah and Zalmunna. Without their kings, the Midianites were helpless. They were so frightened that Gideon and his men easily destroyed them.

Then they headed back where they came from. On the way they stopped at the town of Succoth.

"Well," said Gideon, "we're back, and we've got Zebah and Zalmunna with us! Do you remember how you refused to feed us when we were hungry? Do you remember what you said to us?"

He found the seventy-seven leaders of the town and beat all of them with desert thorns and briars.

Next they went to Penuel. They tore down the tower and killed the men of the city.

After taking revenge on those towns, Gideon turned to Zebah and Zalmunna, the Midianite kings. He wanted to get even with them, too.

"Tell me something," he said. "Tell me about the men you killed at Tabor. What did they look like?"

"Why, they looked just like you!" answered the kings, and they described the men they had killed.

"Just as I thought!" said Gideon. "Those were my brothers, the sons of my mother! As the Lord lives, if you hadn't killed them, I wouldn't kill you now!"

He said to his oldest son, Jether, "Go on, kill these men who murdered your uncles!"

But Jether was only a boy and he was afraid.

"Come on! Kill us yourself!" said Zebah and Zalmunna. "It takes a man to do a man's job!"

After Gideon killed the two kings, the Midianites were completely defeated. They stayed out in the desert, far from the land of Canaan, and they never bothered the Israelites again.

The Israelites were so grateful to Gideon, they came to him and said, "Be our king! We want you and your sons after you, and their sons after them, to rule over us, for you have saved us from the power of the Midianites!"

"No," answered Gideon, "I won't be your king, and neither will my sons. The Lord is your king! But there's one thing you can do for me. I noticed that the Midianites wear gold earrings like all the desert people. Wen I killed Zebah and Zalmunna, I took some beautiful chains from their camels. I'd like to have more Midianite gold. Give me any gold earrings that you took from them."

"We'll be glad to give them to you," the people answered.

Gideon spread out his cloak, and the Israelites threw the Midianite earrings onto it. He collected about forty pounds of gold.

He took the gold and made it into a beautiful charm which he set up in Ophrah for all the people to see. This image became a trap for Gideon and his family and the other Israelites. They began to worship it, and soon they were back to their evil ways.

But for a while the land was at peace, and as

long as Gideon lived, the Lord kept the Israelites safe from their enemies. Gideon lived at his home in Ophrah for forty more years, happy with his many wives and children.

19

The Worthless King

Judges 8—9

ONE of Gideon's wives was a servant girl from Shechem. She and Gideon had a son named Abimelech (meaning "my father is king"). But Abimelech grew up to be the wrong kind of king.

After Gideon died, the Israelites ignored his family. They were ungrateful to them for all the good that Gideon had done. They were also unfaithful to the Lord. They ignored the God who had rescued them from their enemies. They worshiped idols instead.

In the city of Shechem, the very place where

the Israelites had promised to obey the Lord, they built a temple to Baal. And when they broke the covenant with the Lord, they made a covenant with Baal.

One day Gideon's son Abimelech went to the city of Shechem to visit his mother's brothers.

"Please give the leaders of your city a message," he said to his uncles. "Ask them if they would let me be their king. Remind them that I am the only one of Gideon's seventy sons who has relatives in Shechem."

Abimelech's uncles took his message to the leaders of Shechem, and they listened carefully. Abimelech their king? It might be a good idea. It would certainly be better than being ruled by all seventy of Gideon's sons. "After all," they said, "Abimelech is our relative!"

They gave Abimelech seventy pieces of silver from the temple of Baal. He used the silver to hire some town loafers and thugs to follow him. He led them to the city of Ophrah, where they murdered his brothers. They killed all of them on a single stone block. Only Jotham, the youngest of the seventy, got away.

Then the leaders of Shechem met and decided to make Abimelech their king. Beneath the sacred oak tree at Shechem they anointed Abimelech with oil, the usual way to make someone a king.

When Jotham heard what was going on, he came out of his hiding place and went to

Shechem. He stood on Mount Gerizim and shouted, "People of Shechem! If you want God's blessing, listen to me!"

Then Jotham told the people a fable. This simple story had a hidden meaning, a warning for Shechem.

"Once upon a time," said Jotham, "the trees decided they needed a king. So they said to the olive tree, 'Be our king and rule over us.'

"But the olive tree answered, 'Why should I stop making olive oil, which is useful to people, just to wave back and forth over you?'

"Next the trees asked the fig tree, 'Come, be our king!'

But the fig tree answered, 'Why should I stop making sweet figs, which are valuable to people, just to wave back and forth over you? There's no use in that!'"

"Then the trees said to the grape vine, 'Come, you be our king!'

"But for the third time, they received 'no' for an answer. The grape vine said, 'Why should I stop making my wine, which cheers the hearts of people, to do something as worthless as swaying over you?'

"Finally, the trees spoke to the thornbush, a useless plant which makes no oil or fruit or wine. 'Come, you be our king!'

"The prickly thornbush answered, 'If you really want me to be your king, then come, find protection in my shade! But I warn you. If you're not honest in making this covenant with me, then fire will break out from my thorny branches and burn up all the trees—even the mighty cedars of Lebanon!'"

When Jotham finished the story, he warned, "Leaders of Shechem, if you're making an honest agreement with Abimelech, all right. If you've been fair to Gideon's family, all right. But you've turned against my father's family. He risked his life to fight for you against the Midianites, and you murdered his sons! And now you've made Abimelech your king. If that's honest and fair, you'll be happy. But if it isn't, you will be cursed with fire. May fire come blazing out of

Abimelech and destroy you! May fire destroy your fortress and the temple of your idol! And may fire come blazing out of you and destroy Abimelech!"

And with this curse, Jotham finished speaking and ran away. He was so afraid of his brother that he never came back. He settled in a town far from the reach of Abimelech.

20

Jotham's Curse Comes True

Judges 9

FOR the next three years Abimelech ruled over Shechem and the neighboring towns. Then God sent a spirit of hatred between Abimelech and the leaders of Shechem. He did this to punish them for the murder of Gideon's sons.

Shechem stood at a pass between Mount Ebal and Mount Gerizim. Many caravans traveled through the pass, paying tolls to Abimelech as king of Shechem. The leaders of Shechem put men in ambush on the mountaintops to rob the travelers as they passed by on the highway near the city. They posted lookouts to watch for Abimelech while they made their raids. When the raiders frightened away the caravans, Abimelech lost the money from the tolls.

Then a man named Gaal came to Shechem with a group of followers. The leaders of Shechem trusted him, and Gaal began to think that he could take Abimelech's place as king.

One day the men of the city went to their vineyards to pick grapes. They made wine from the grapes and went into the temple of their god Baal to celebrate the harvest. They ate and drank and began to talk against Abimelech. They hated him.

They bragged about the raids on the caravans. They knew this annoyed Abimelech, even though Abimelech hadn't done anything about it. Maybe he was afraid of them!

"Who is Abimelech, anyway?" asked Gaal. "Why should people like us take orders from him and his commander Zebul? It would be better if they served us. I'm not a foreigner like Abimelech. Both my parents are from Shechem. If I ruled this city, the first thing I'd do would be to get rid of Abimelech. I'd tell him! I'd say, 'Hey, Abimelech, you've been here long enough! Get your men and get out of town.'"

Zebul, Abimelech's commander in Shechem, heard about the party in the temple. He was furious. He sent messengers to Abimelech, who was with his men at a nearby town.

"Listen!" said Zebul. "Gaal and his men are here in Shechem, stirring up the city against you! Come and attack him with all your might!"

Abimelech and his men came to Shechem that night, as Zebul had advised. They hid in the fields around the city.

The next morning Gaal came out and stood by the city gate. When Abimelech saw him, he and his men got up from their hiding places.

"Look!" said Gaal to Zebul, "I see men coming down from the hilltops!"

"Those aren't men," answered Zebul. "You see the shadow of the mountains. They just look like men moving across the fields."

But Gaal kept watching.

"Look!" he said again. "I do see men! Over there! There are more of them! They're moving in the fields all around the city!"

"Aha!" cried Zebul. "Those *are* men, Gaal! Abimelech's men! And it's too late for you to do anything about it. Where's your brave talk now, Gaal? You bragged you'd get rid of Abimelech. Well, here's your chance!"

Then Zebul watched while Gaal led the men of Shechem out to fight Abimelech.

Abimelech and his men killed many of Gaal's men and chased the others all the way back to the city gate. Abimelech captured the city and destroyed everything in it. Then he spread salt on the ground as a curse.

Gaal and his men escaped, and no one ever heard of them again.

As soon as the battle was lost and the people of the city were killed, the leaders of Shechem went and hid in the tower of the temple of their god.

Abimelech found out where they were hiding, but he realized that the tower was too strong for him to capture. It was a fortress with thick stone walls. So he and his men took some axes and climbed up the side of Mount Ebal. There Abimelech cut bundles of firewood from the trees. He picked up the branches and put them on his shoulder.

"Hurry!" he told his men. "Take these axes and do the same!"

They cut down branches and carried the

bundles back down the mountainside. They went straight to the fortress at Shechem and piled the wood up around it. Then they set it on fire, destroying the fortress and all the people inside, about a thousand men and women.

After that, Abimelech went to Thebez, a town about ten miles outside of Shechem. When he and his men surrounded the town, the people of Thebez shut themselves inside their fortress. They locked the door behind them and climbed up to the roof of the tower.

Abimelech went up to the door of the fortress, ready to destroy it with fire, just as he had done at Shechem.

But before he could light the wood, a woman who was standing on the roof of the tower pushed a heavy stone down on top of him. It hit Abimelech's head and fractured his skull.

As he lay dying, Abimelech groaned to his servant, "Take a sword and kill me. Let no one say I was killed by a woman."

So the servant killed Abimelech. When the people saw that their king was dead, they all went back to their homes.

And that is how the curse of Jotham came true, and the Lord punished the crime against Gideon and his sons.

The Outlaw Chief and His Terrible Vow

Judges 10—11

AFTER the death of Abimelech, the Lord again sent judges to save Israel. Tola, a man from the tribe of Issachar, was judge for twenty-three years. Jair, a man from Gilead, was judge for twenty-two years.

But then the Israelites went back to worshiping idols and doing wicked things again. They bowed down to Baal and Asherah and also to the gods of the Syrians, the Phoenicians, the Moabites, the Ammonites, and the Philistines.

The Lord was so angry with his people that he

turned them over to the Ammonites. The Ammonites came from Ammon into Gilead and annoyed the Israelites in Gilead for eighteen years. Then they crossed the Jordan River and attacked the tribes of Judah, Benjamin, and Ephraim.

Finally, the Israelites cried out to the Lord, "We've sinned against you! We've left you, the Lord our God, and we've worshiped idols instead!"

The Lord answered, "I saved you from the Egyptians and I saved you from the Canaanites. I sent judges to rescue you from your enemies. I could easily save you from these Ammonites. But you've left me to serve other gods, so I'm not going to save you anymore. Go, pray to the gods you have chosen. Let them save you this time!"

"Please, Lord," prayed the Israelites, "We're sorry. Please save us!"

They got rid of their idols and began to worship the Lord, so he had mercy on them and answered their prayers.

While they were waiting for the Lord to save them, the Israelites became frightened. The Ammonites were gathering a great army in Gilead, and the leaders of the eastern tribes didn't know what to do.

They called all their soldiers to meet at a place called Mizpah.

"Who will lead us against the Ammonites?" they asked. No one was brave enough to start the battle.

"Whoever strikes the first blow at the Ammonites can become chief of all Gilead!" promised the leaders. But still no one wanted to do it.

The situation was very dangerous, for the Ammonites were about to attack. The leaders of Gilead sent to the land of Tob for help.

A great warrior named Jephthah had left Gilead many years before. He was the son of a servant girl, and he had run away after his half-brothers, the sons of his father's wife, had forced him out of their home. He became the leader of an outlaw band, and other outcasts joined him to go raiding. This bandit chief was the only man in Gilead who wasn't afraid of the Ammonites.

"Come, please lead us!" said the leaders of Gilead to Jephthah. "We need you to attack the Ammonites."

"Why are you coming to me?" he asked. "You're the same men who forced me out of Gilead. You're here now just because you're in trouble."

"Please," they begged. "We need you! Please come with us. If you lead us in battle, we'll make you our ruler, chief of all the people in Gilead!"

"Why should I believe you?" asked Jephthah. Then he thought it over. "If the Lord gives me victory, will you really let me be your ruler?"

"Yes, yes!" they promised. "We swear it. May the Lord be our witness. That's exactly what we'll do!"

So Jephthah agreed to go back with them to Gilead, and they made him commander of their army.

Jephthah made a solemn promise to the Lord. He vowed to lead the Israelites against the Ammonites if they would make him ruler of Gilead.

Then he sent messengers to the king of the Ammonites, to see if they could settle the quarrel peacefully.

"You're gathering an army against us," said Jephthah. "You claim that this land of Gilead belongs to you. But the Lord, the God of Israel, gave us this land. Where have you been all these years while the Israelites have been settling in this land? It's too late for you to claim it! You've conquered some land from Moab—well, let Chemosh, god of the Moabites, conquer land for you!"

The king of the Ammonites ignored Jephthah's message. He continued to gather his soldiers to attack the Israelites.

Then the spirit of the Lord came over Jephthah, and he went through the territory of Gilead and Manasseh to find soldiers to join him.

Then he returned to Mizpah and made another vow to the Lord. "If you give me victory over the Ammonites," Jephthah promised, "when I return home, I'll sacrifice to you the first creature that comes out to meet me!"

Jephthah led the Israelites against the Ammonites, and the Lord gave him victory. He

thoroughly defeated the enemy.

After the battle Jephthah returned to his home at Mizpah. He remembered his promise to sacrifice the first creature that came out to meet him. Sheep or goat or whatever, he would offer it to the Lord to thank him for the victory.

But what did he see coming out to meet him? His only child—his lovely daughter! She was playing the tambourine and dancing.

"Oh, no!" cried Jephthah. "My daughter! You're breaking my heart. I've made a promise to the Lord, and I must keep it."

He tore his clothes in sorrow.

"Father," said Jephthah's daughter. "If you made a promise to the Lord, do what you must, for the Lord has defeated your enemies. Just let me go into the hills with my friends for a while first to cry because I'll die unmarried and without children!"

"Go!" he said.

Jephthah's daughter and her friends went into the hills to mourn, and after two months she returned to her father and he kept his promise.

Jephthah didn't understand that the Lord never wants human sacrifice. The Canaanites often sacrificed their children to idols. Many Israelites had forgotten the teaching of God and they copied the horrible customs of their neighbors. This was the kind of terrible thing that happened when God's people worshiped idols.

22

"Say 'Shibboleth'!"

Judges 12

SOON after Jephthah lost his daughter, the men of Ephraim came to Gilead with a complaint. They wanted to join the fight against the Ammonites, but it was too late. They were angry and they shouted at Jephthah.

"Why did you fight without us?" they demanded. Ephraim was the largest and most powerful of all the tribes of Israel. They weren't used to being ignored.

"We'll punish you!" they threatened. "We'll burn your house down on top of your head!"

113

"Please," said Jephthah. "I tried to work things out peacefully, but the Ammonites wouldn't listen. I called for help, but you didn't come, so I took my life in my hands and went into Ammon without you. The Lord has defeated the Ammonites, so why are you here? To fight with me?"

"Traitors!" shouted the Ephraimites. "You people over here on the east side of the Jordan are deserters from Israel!"

Then there was war between the men of Gilead and the men of Ephraim. Jephthah's army defeated the Ephraimites and chased them back toward the Jordan River.

When they got to the shallow crossing places of

the Jordan, the Ephraimites found soldiers from Gilead waiting for them.

"Are you from Ephraim?" asked the Gileadites.

"No," they lied.

"Say 'Shibboleth!' " demanded the Gileadites.

"Sibboleth!" said the Ephraimites. The people from Ephraim couldn't pronounce that Hebrew word correctly, so the soldiers knew they were Ephraimites.

The Gileadites captured and killed forty-two companies of Ephraimites. That tribe was never so powerful in Israel again.

Jephthah lived for six more years, and he judged Israel until he died.

Then the Lord sent three more judges. Ibzan of the tribe of Asher was judge for seven years, Elon of the tribe of Zebulun was judge for ten years, and Abdon of the tribe of Ephraim was judge for eight years. So there was peace in the land for twenty-five more years.

23

A Mysterious Visitor

Judges 13

THE next time the Israelites sinned against the Lord, he let the Philistines rule over them for forty years. These were the powerful people who lived on the seacoast. They knew the secret of making iron tools and weapons, and they worshiped a god named Dagon.

In those days a man named Manoah lived in the town of Zorah in the territory of the tribe of Dan, near the Philistines.

One day a mysterious stranger appeared to Manoah's wife.

"Listen to me!" he said. "You've never been able to have children, but soon you'll have a baby. From now on, don't drink wine or beer or eat any forbidden food. Your child will begin the work of rescuing the Israelites from the Philistines."

The woman went to her husband. "A man of God just came to me!" she said. "He looked as holy as an angel. I didn't ask him where he came from, and he didn't tell me his name, but he said I am going to have a baby!"

When Manoah heard what had happened, he prayed, "Please, Lord, let the man of God come back to us! Have him tell us what we must do with this child when he is born."

The Lord answered Manoah's prayer. A few days later his wife was sitting alone in the field when she saw the stranger again. She ran quickly to Manoah. "Come at once! The man of God is here again!"

Manoah got up and followed her out to the field.

"Are you the one who spoke to my wife?"

"I am."

"Well, may your words come true! Please tell us what we must do for the boy. How should he live?"

"Your child will be under a special vow to the Lord, and he must follow the rules of the Nazirites all his life. He must never drink wine or beer or eat forbidden food. He must never cut his hair. If he follows these rules until the day of his death, the Lord will be with him!"

"Please don't go now," said Manoah. "Stay with us, sir. Let us cook a young goat for you."

"If I stay, I won't eat your food," said the stranger, "but go ahead and cook it. You can burn it as an offering to the Lord."

"Tell us, what is your name?" asked Manoah. "When your words come true, we'll honor you!"

"Why do you ask my name? It's a mystery you cannot understand."

Then Manoah took the young goat and some

grain and offered them on a rock altar as a sacrifice to the Lord.

As the flame of the burning offering went up from the altar, Manoah and his wife saw a miracle. The stranger went up toward heaven in the flames!

They realized then that the stranger was the angel of the Lord, and they bowed down to the ground in worship.

"We'll die," whispered Manoah to his wife. "We've seen God!"

"No," she said. "If the Lord wanted to kill us, why did he accept our offering? Why did he tell us those things about the baby?"

They never saw the angel again, but after some time Manoah and his wife had a baby boy. They named him Samson, and as he grew, the Lord blessed him.

One day while Samson was visiting an army camp near Zorah, the spirit of the Lord began to make him strong and powerful.

24

Samson and the Girl from Timnah

Judges 14

ONE day Samson went down to the Philistine city of Timnah, a few miles from his home. While he was there, he noticed a Philistine girl. He came home and told his mother and father, "I saw a woman at Timnah, one of the Philistines. Get her for me. I want to marry her."

"That's a terrible idea!" said Samson's parents. "Why should you marry one of those heathen? There are lots of nice girls in your own tribe!"

"I want that one!" he answered. "Get her for me!"

Samson's parents didn't realize it, but the Lord was looking for an excuse for Samson to fight the Philistines.

Samson went back to Timnah. On the way he left the road and went into a vineyard. Suddenly, a young lion came roaring toward him.

The spirit of the Lord came over Samson, making him strong, and he tore the lion open with his bare hands.

Samson went on to Timnah and talked to the girl. He liked her even more than before. *She's the right one for me*, he thought.

A while later he went back to see her again. On the way, he left the road and went into the vineyard to look at the remains of the dead lion. Inside the carcass he found a bees' nest and some honey.

Samson scooped some honey out with his hands and ate it as he walked along. When he got home, he gave his parents some, but he didn't tell them about the lion.

Samson decided to marry the girl. When he went down to Timnah for the wedding, the girl's father gave a great feast at his house. The party lasted for a week. The Philistines invited thirty young men to stay with Samson, and they amused themselves with jokes and riddles.

On the first day of the wedding feast Samson said to the young men, "Let me ask you a riddle. I'll bet you can't tell me the answer before the end of the feast. If you do, I'll give each of you a fine new robe!"

"Tell us!" they said. "Come on! We're listening."
Samson said,

> Out of the eater came something to eat.
> And out of the strong came something sweet.
> What is it?"

Three days later the young men were still trying to figure out Samson's riddle.

On the fourth day they went to his bride. "Did
you invite us to this party to rob us?" they asked
her. "Find out the answer to your husband's rid-

dle, or we'll set fire to your father's house and burn all of you up!"

Samson's wife went to him and cried on his shoulder. "You don't love me," she said. "You hate me. You told my friends a riddle, and you didn't tell me the answer!"

"Now look here," said Samson, "I haven't even told my father and mother. Why should I tell you?"

But she kept on crying, and she cried for the rest of the week. Finally, on the last day of the feast, Samson gave in to her teasing. He told her how he had killed the lion with his bare hands and how later he had found the honey in the lion's body.

She went straight to the thirty young men and told them the answer to the riddle.

Just as the sun was going down that evening, the young men went to Samson. He was standing by the door of his bride's room. They asked,

> What is sweeter than honey?
> What is stronger than a lion?

Samson was furious. He cried,

> If you hadn't plowed with my young cow,
> You woudn't know the answer now!

Then the Spirit of the Lord came over Samson, making him strong. He went down to the Philistine city of Ashkelon and killed thirty men. He took their fine robes and brought them back and gave them to the thirty men at the feast. Leaving his wife behind, he returned to Zorah, burning with anger.

25

Foxes' Tails and a Donkey's Jawbone

Judges 15

WHEN Samson cooled down, he went back to Timnah to visit his wife. He took a young goat to give her as a present.

His father-in-law met him at the door.

"Let me in," said Samson. "I want to see my wife."

But the girl's father blocked the way.

"You were so angry, I thought you hated her," he said. "I thought you were divorcing her, so after you left, I gave her to another man. But wait! Don't be upset! She has a nice younger sister. Wouldn't you rather have her? Here, take her instead."

"No!" said Samson, and he left. He walked away muttering, "I'm going to get even with those Philistines! I'll pay them back for this!"

He went out and caught three hundred foxes. He tied them together in pairs by their tails and put torches between the knots. He lit the torches and turned the foxes loose in the fields of the Philistines.

It was the season of the wheat harvest, and as the foxes ran howling through the fields, the torches on their tails set the ripe wheat on fire. Then the foxes ran through the vineyards and olive groves so that all the Philistines' crops were completely destroyed.

When they saw what had happened, the Philistines said to each other, "Who has done this awful thing?"

"Samson," was the answer, "because his father-in-law gave his wife to another man."

So some Philistines went to the house of Samson's father-in-law and burned it down, with all the people in it.

Samson heard about this, and he became even more furious. "You won't get away with this!" he cried. "I won't rest until I have my revenge!"

He attacked the Philistines with all his strength, killing many of them. Then he went to the hill country of Judah and hid in a cave at Etam Cliff.

Soon an army of Philistines came to the territory of Judah, looking for Samson. After they made camp, they raided a town near Etam.

"Why are you attacking us?" asked the men of Judah.

"We're after Samson," answered the Philistines. "We want to take him prisoner and pay him back for what he did to us."

Three companies of men from Judah went out to the cave where Samson was hiding. "Don't you realize that the Philistines have us in their power?" they asked him. "You make them angry, and we have to suffer!"

"I was just paying them back," he answered. "I was only doing to them what they did to me!"

"Well, we're here to take you prisoner. We're going to hand you over to the Philistines so they won't hurt us."

"Just promise me one thing," said Samson. "Don't kill me yourselves."

"All right," they answered. "We don't want to kill you anyway."

They tied him up with two new ropes and took him to the Philistine camp. When the Philistines saw their enemy tied up, they came out running and shouting with joy. But before they could grab him, the spirit of the Lord came over Samson and strengthened him. He broke the ropes on his arms like thread!

Then he took the first weapon he could find, a donkey's jawbone that was lying on the ground. The bone was fresh and strong, and Samson swung it left and right like a club. He struck down a whole company of Philistines.

Samson was so happy, he made up a song and sang it right there.

> With the jawbone of an ass,
> I've piled them a mass!

Then he threw the bone away. He was exhausted.

"I'm thirsty," Samson prayed. "This is your victory, Lord. You won it through me. Now will you save me from dying of thirst? I'm too weak to get away from here!"

God opened up a hollow in the ground and water gushed out. Samson drank until his strength returned and he felt lively again.

26

Samson and Delilah

Judges 16

SAMSON was a judge in Israel for twenty years, and during that time he had many exciting adventures.

One day he went down to the Philistine city of Gaza, where he met a woman and went into her house. When the men of Gaza found out that their enemy was in the city, they shut the gates to trap him inside.

"We'll wait until morning," they said. "He can't get out of this walled city alive!"

But Samson came at midnight and took hold of

the city gate and pulled it up out of the ground—doors, posts, lock, and all! He lifted the enormous gate onto his shoulders and carried it all the way to the city of Hebron, forty miles away! He left the Gaza gate on a hill outside Hebron.

The Philistines waited all night in the tower by the city gate. In the morning they discovered that Samson was gone—and so was their gate!

Samson fell in love again, this time with a woman named Delilah who lived in the Valley of Sorek, between the hills of Judah and the land of the Philistines.

When they found out about Samson and Delilah, the rulers of the five Philistine cities went to visit Delilah. "Help us catch Samson," they said. "Find out what makes him so strong, and how we could overpower him and tie him up to make him helpless. If you do this, we'll give you eleven hundred pieces of silver!"

Delilah agreed to help them. When Samson came to visit her the next time, she asked him, "Please tell me what makes you so strong. How could someone tie you up and make you helpless?"

He answered, "If someone tied me up with seven new bowstrings that weren't dried out, well, then I'd be as weak as anybody else!"

When the five Philistine rulers came back, Delilah told them what Samson had said. They brought her the bowstrings, and then they hid in another room of her house.

Samson came to visit, and while he was sleeping, Delilah tied him up. Then she shouted, "Samson! The Philistines are coming!"

He jumped up and yanked off the cords like threads snapping in a fire. The Philistines sneaked away, and Samson kept the secret of his strength.

Then Delilah said, "Look, Samson! You made a fool of me and told me lies. Now please tell me how you can be tied up."

Samson was enjoying himself. He didn't realize what a deadly game he was playing.

"If someone tied me up with new ropes that have never been used, I'd be as weak as anybody else," he teased.

Delilah got the ropes and hid the Philistines in the other room. Again, she tied Samson up while he slept.

"Samson!" she shouted. "The Philistines are coming!"

But for the second time Samson snapped off the ropes like thread.

"You're still making a fool of me," complained Delilah. "You're telling me lies. Now really tell me how to tie you up!"

He thought a minute, and then he noticed the loom on the other side of the room. There was a piece of half-woven material in it.

"If someone wove my hair into the loom like thread, right into the cloth, then I would be as weak as anybody!"

Delilah lulled Samson to sleep next to the loom, and then she wove his long hair into the cloth. She fastened it to the side of the loom with a peg.

After he was tied to the loom, Delilah shouted, "Samson! The Philistines are coming!"

He woke up, yanked his hair loose, and broke free from the loom. For the third time his secret was safe.

"How can you say you love me, when you don't trust me?" teased Delilah. "Three times now you've made a fool of me. You still haven't told me what makes you so strong."

Day after day she nagged him until finally Samson got so sick and tired of it that he told her the truth.

"My hair has never been cut," Samson explained. "I've been dedicated to God since before I was born. If I cut my hair, then the Lord will take away my strength and I'll be as weak as everybody else."

Delilah realized that Samson was telling the truth. She sent for the Philistine rulers. "Come at once! He has told me the real secret of his strength!"

They came with the eleven hundred pieces of silver they had promised her.

Delilah hid the Philistines in the next room and then she lulled Samson to sleep on her lap. She motioned to a servant to bring her a razor to cut off Samson's hair.

"Samson!" she shouted when his hair was gone. "The Philistines are coming!"

Samson jumped up just as the Philistines came bursting into the room. He tried to get away, not realizing that the Lord had left him. He was as weak as anybody else, and they captured him.

The five Philistine rulers overpowered Samson and gouged out his eyes. Then they took him down to Gaza and tied him up with bronze chains. They put him to work turning the millstone in the prison, like a blind donkey.

Day after day in the Philistine prison Samson slaved like an animal. And day after day Samson's hair grew.

One day the Philistine rulers called their people together for a celebration. They said:

> Our god has given into our hand
> Samson, the enemy of our land!

They offered a great sacrifice to their god Dagon and sang praises to him.

> Samson set fire to our
>   fields and then
> He swung a jawbone
>   and killed our men.
> Now Dagon has given him
>   into our hand—
> Samson, the enemy
>   of our land!

While they were feasting and enjoying themselves, someone called out, "Go get Samson.

133

Bring him up here to entertain us."

When Samson was brought up from the prison and the Philistines saw how blind and helpless he was, they laughed at him. They thought Dagon was more powerful than the God of the Israelites.

Samson turned to the boy who was leading him by the hand. "Put me in a place where I can touch the pillars that hold up this building," he said. "I want to lean on them."

The temple of Dagon was crowded with people, including all five of the Philistine rulers. On the roof stood about three thousand more men and women, all of them making fun of Samson.

As he stood between the pillars he could hear their cruel shouts. "Lord God," he prayed, "please remember me. Please, God! Give me back my strength. Just this once! Let me pay back the Philistines for my eyes."

He put his right arm around one pillar and his left arm around the other.

"Let me die with the Philistines!" he shouted.

Then he pushed and pulled with all his strength, and the building came crashing down on top of Samson and the rulers and all the Philistines.

Samson's brothers came down to get his body. They took it back and buried it in the tomb of his father Manoah. At his death Samson killed more Philistines than during his whole life.

27

A Thief and His Idols

Judges 17

Once there was a woman who lived in the hill country of Ephraim. She had eleven hundred pieces of silver, and one day someone took them. She swore an oath, cursing the thief.

A little while later her son, a man named Micah, came to her and said, "I heard you swear an oath about the silver you lost. Well, I have it. Here it is. I'm giving it back to you."

"May the Lord bless you, my son!" she said. She didn't want her son to be cursed, so she promised, "I'll dedicate the silver to the Lord."

But instead of taking the silver to the tabernacle at Shiloh, the woman kept most of it for herself. She gave two hundred pieces of the eleven hundred to a metal worker to melt down and make into an image.

Then Micah's mother gave the idol to Micah, and he put it in his house and worshiped it. He built a special place in his house called a shrine and put some little idols and charms next to the big silver image. Then he asked one of his sons to be the priest in his shrine.

This was against God's teaching, against the Ten Commandments, but in those days most people in Israel had forgotten God's laws. They didn't do what God wanted them to do, but they did whatever they pleased. They worshiped idols and said they were worshiping the Lord. They lied, cheated, and stole. They didn't love the Lord and they didn't love each other. They behaved like the pagans who lived all around them.

One day a young man from the tribe of Levi came to the hill country of Ephraim. His name was Jonathan. He was a Levite, a member of the tribe of priests who had no land of their own.

When Jonathan came to Micah's village, Micah asked him, "Where do you come from?"

"I'm a Levite from Bethlehem in Judah," Jonathan answered. "I'm looking for a place to settle."

"Stay here with me," said Micah. "I could use a real priest. I have a beautiful shrine in my house with a wonderful silver image. Come, be my priest, and I'll give you ten pieces of silver a year and clothes and food and a place to stay. I'll take good care of you!"

Jonathan agreed to stay, and Micah treated him like a son.

Micah was pleased with himself. "Now I've got a Levite for my priest," he said. "The Lord will give me everything I ask for and do whatever I want!"

He had no idea how wrong he was.

Justice for Idol Worshipers

Judges 18

AT the same time that Micah was hiring Jonathan to be his priest, the people from the tribe of Dan were looking for a place to live. They had settled near Judah, but they needed more room, because the Philistines were crowding them.

The Danites chose five brave men and sent them out from the towns of Zorah and Eshtaol as spies. The spies explored the land, looking for a new place for their tribe to settle.

When they came to the hill country of Eph-

139

raim, the spies happened to find Micah's house. It was the custom for strangers to stay in homes, so they spent the night there.

In the morning the five men met Jonathan. They could tell from his accent that he was from Judah.

"How did you get here?" they asked him. "What are you doing in this place?"

"I work for Micah," he explained. "We have an agreement. I'm his priest and he gives me everything I need!"

"Well, then, since you're a priest, do something for us. Ask God if we're going to be successful in our mission."

Jonathan went to the shrine to find out from the idols and charms what would happen in the future.

"You have nothing to worry about," he reported back to them. "You'll find a good place to settle and the Lord will give you everything you need."

The five spies left Micah's house and went north until they came to a city called Laish. The people of Laish were quiet and peaceful. There was no wall around their city.

The spies went back to their tribe.

"What did you see?" the Danites asked them. "Tell us all about it."

"We found a very good place," they answered. "It's a rich city with peaceful people. Come on! Let's go attack them right now! Don't just sit here! They're Phoenicians, but they're too far from Sidon or another Phoenician city for anyone to help them. Come on!"

Six hundred armed men and their families left Dan. They camped first in Judah and then went on their way through the hills of Ephraim until they came to Micah's house.

The five men who had spied out the land said to the others, "Let's stop here. There are gods in that house—a beautiful silver image and charms. We could make good use of those!"

They went into the house and greeted Jonathan while the soldiers waited outside. Then Jonathan went out and stood with the soldiers.

A few minutes later the five men came out of Micah's house, carrying the silver idol, the charms, and the little carved images.

"What are you doing?" asked Jonathan.

"Keep quiet," they answered. "Put your hand over your mouth. Come with us, and you can be our priest. Wouldn't you rather be priest for a whole tribe than for just one man's family?"

Jonathan was so pleased with the idea that he went along with them, marching right in the middle of the soldiers.

A little while later Micah came home and discovered the robbery. He called his neighbors to help him, and they chased after the thieves from Dan, running and shouting at them.

The Danites turned around. "What's the matter with you?" asked one of the soldiers. "What's all this shouting about?"

"You took away the god that I made!" said Micah. "You took away my priest! I don't have anything left! How can you ask what's the matter?"

"Don't shout," warned the soldier. "If I hear any more out of you, you'll find out that some of these fellows with me have very nasty tempers! If they get mad, they'll attack you and your family."

Micah realized that the Danites were too strong for him, so he turned around and went home.

The people of Dan went on their way. When

they got to Laish, they attacked the city and killed the peaceful people who lived there. Nobody came to help Laish, and the Danites burned the city. On that same spot they built a new city and settled there. They called their city Dan, a name which means "justice," after their ancestor, the son of Jacob.

In the city of Dan they built a temple for Micah's idols. They made Jonathan their priest, and when he died, his sons became Dan's priests.

For many years the idol temple stood at Dan, with Jonathan's family as priests. Other Israelites living in the north copied the people of Dan and came to the idol temple to worship. This terrible behavior kept up until enemies came and carried them away from the land forever.

That was God's justice for the idol worshipers.

29

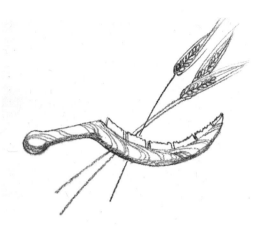

The Crime at Gibeah

Judges 19

IN those days when most Israelites had forgotten God's laws, many terrible things happened. The people worshiped idols and did wicked things to each other. Sometimes God sent judges to help the people, to teach them, and to free them from their enemies. Other times there were no judges, and the Israelites became impatient.

One year there was a horrible crime in Israel, and instead of waiting for God's justice, the Israelites took matters into their own hands. The result was civil war.

It began with a Levite who had a problem. His wife became angry with him. She left their home in the far hills of Ephraim and returned to her father's house in Bethlehem.

After four months the Levite decided to try to win her back. He took his servant and two donkeys and set out on a journey.

When he arrived at Bethlehem, his father-in-law came out to meet him. He was glad to see his son-in-law, and he invited him to visit a while. The man agreed to stay for three days.

They ate and drank and had a good time. Then on the morning of the fourth day the Levite prepared to leave. "Have something to eat first," said his father-in-law.

So they sat down and began eating and drinking again. After a while the Levite rose to go, but his father-in-law said, "Spend another night! Don't leave yet. Stay and have a good time!"

So he spent another night there.

On the morning of the fifth day, the Levite again prepared to go, and again his father-in-law said, "Have a bite to eat. Stay and enjoy yourself!" He stayed until late afternoon. Then he stood up and got ready to go.

"Look," said his father-in-law. "It's almost dark. You might as well spend another night here. Enjoy yourself! You can get up early tomorrow morning and leave then."

But this time the Levite refused to stay. Even though it was late, he took his wife and his servant and the two donkeys and headed north, back toward his home in the hills of Ephraim.

It was almost dark when they came to the outskirts of the city of Jerusalem.

"Please, sir," said the servant. "Let's go into this city and spend the night."

"No," answered the Levite. "This is a Jebusite city. I'm not going to stay with foreigners. Those people aren't Israelites. I'm not going to depend on them for hospitality. We'll stay on the road until we get to an Israelite town."

So they went on past Jerusalem until they came to the town of Gibeah in the territory of the tribe of Benjamin. The sun was setting as they turned off the road.

In that part of the world darkness comes quickly after sunset, so it was nighttime when they got to Gibeah. Hotels and inns were rare, and most people stayed in homes when they traveled. Taking strangers in was a sacred duty, and guests were honored above members of the family.

The Levite sat down in the city square and waited for someone to offer them a place to stay. No one did. Everyone in Gibeah ignored him.

Then an old man came in from his day's work in the fields outside town. He saw the strangers in the square, but unlike everyone else in Gibeah, he went up to them.

"Where did you come from? Where are you going?" he asked.

"We're just passing through on our way from Bethlehem to the hills of Ephraim," answered the Levite. "We have enough straw and food for the donkeys, and bread and wine for ourselves. We just need a place to sleep, but no one has invited us."

"You're welcome in my house," said the old man. "I'm not a member of the tribe of Benjamin. I'm like you, from the hills of Ephraim. Let me take care of everything. But whatever you do, don't spend the night out here in the open!"

He took them home and let them wash their feet while he fed the donkeys. Then he invited them to eat. While they were enjoying themselves, some rough men from the town, devilish characters, came and surrounded the house.

They beat their fists on the door and shouted, "Bring out that stranger! Let us have him!"

The old man went out. "No, my friends! Please! Leave this man alone. He's my guest! Look, here's my young daughter. I'll send her out to you. But don't touch this stranger!"

The men of Gibeah ignored the old man and kept pounding on the door. The Levite was terrified, so he took his wife and pushed her out the door. The men of Gibeah took her and abused her all night.

Just before sunrise they left and the woman came and fell down at the doorstep. When the Levite opened the door she was still there, lying in front of the house, with her hands reaching for the door. "Get up," he said. "It's time to go."

But she made no answer, for she was dead.

The Levite lifted his wife's body and laid her across the back of one of the donkeys. When he reached home, he took a knife and cut the body into twelve pieces. Then he sent messengers with the pieces through all the territory of Israel, one to each tribe.

"See what has happened," the messengers said to everyone they met. "Nothing so terrible as this crime has ever been committed in Israel, not in all the time since we left Egypt! Aren't you going to do something about it?"

"It's horrible!" said everyone who got the message. "We must do something. But what?"

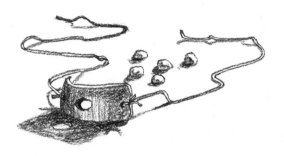

Civil War in Israel

Judges 20

THE men of Israel met together in the territory of Ephraim. They came from every direction—from as far north as Dan, from as far south as Beersheba, and from as far east as Gilead. All the leaders of the tribes came, and four hundred companies of armed men.

"Speak!" said the leaders to the Levite. "Tell us what happened!"

He told them the story of the crime at Gibeah, how the people there refused hospitality and murdered his wife.

"They've done a terrible thing," he cried. "Now what are you going to do about it?"

"We'll form a mighty army!" they answered. "We'll punish Gibeah for this crime!"

They sent a messenger to the town of Gibeah, to see if they could settle the problem without war.

"What are you going to do about this crime?" asked the messenger. "If you hand the criminals over to us, we'll put them to death and remove this evil from Israel!"

But the people of Gibeah would not hand over the criminals. Instead of settling the matter peacefully, they gathered an army of their own from all over the territory of the tribe of

Benjamin. They called out twenty-five companies of swordsmen and a special force of seven hundred slingers who could sling a stone at a piece of hair without missing.

The next morning the army of the other tribes set out for Benjamin. They camped near the town of Gibeah and placed their soldiers in position, ready to attack the town.

The army of Benjamin came out of Gibeah and killed twenty-two of the four hundred companies of soldiers.

The Israelites were upset by this defeat, and at the end of the day they prayed to the Lord. They thought he was with them in this war against their brother tribe, so they prepared to attack.

The second day they marched out again, and again the Benjaminites defeated them. This time they lost eighteen companies of swordsmen.

The Israelites prayed to the Lord again. They didn't eat all day, but fasted until evening and offered sacrifices to the Lord.

"Should we fight another battle with the Benjaminites?" they asked. "Or should we give up?"

"Attack!" answered the Lord. "Tomorrow I'll defeat them."

The next day they put soldiers in ambush all around Gibeah. For the third time they attacked the town. The Benjaminites came out again to fight and left the city unguarded. They killed about thirty of the Israelites on the main road, and the others ran away.

Then the soldiers in ambush rushed out from their hiding places. They ran into Gibeah and captured the town.

The Benjaminites looked back and saw a column of smoke rising from their town. They didn't realize that it was a signal.

The main part of the Israelite army saw the smoke signal and turned around and attacked.

The battle became so fierce that the Benjaminites panicked. They tried to escape to the wilderness, but the Israelites ran after them, striking down eighteen companies of their soldiers.

They chased the men of Benjamin as far as they could, picking off five companies on the highways and two more in the wilderness.

The Lord gave them victory over the Benjaminites, and they killed twenty-five units of about a hundred men each.

But six hundred Benjaminites from the special force got away. They hid in the wilderness at the Rock of Rimmon, and the Israelites went back to Gibeah.

31

Stealing Wives

Judges 21

WHEN the other Israelites planned the war against the tribe of Benjamin, they made a solemn promise to the Lord. They all agreed not to allow their daughters to marry men from Benjamin.

About four months after the end of the civil war, the Israelites met at Shiloh at the tabernacle to pray to the Lord. Shiloh was in the northern hill country. Here all the people gathered several times a year for great festivals.

"O Lord, God of Israel," they cried. "Why has

this bitter thing happened? A whole tribe of Israel has completely died out! We killed all the Benjaminites in battle, and then we went through their territory and destroyed their cities. None of the people of Benjamin are left."

While they were praying, someone came and told them about the six hundred men hiding at the Rock of Rimmon.

Early the next morning they rose and offered sacrifices to the Lord.

"How can we find wives for the Benjaminites who are left?" they asked. "We promised we wouldn't let our daughters marry them. The ones at the Rock of Rimmon are the only ones alive. We don't want the tribe of Benjamin to die out, but who in Israel can marry them?"

Then someone said, "Did everyone join the battle? Were all the men of Israel at the meeting to plan the war?" Someone else remembered that when the roll was called, no one answered from the town of Jabesh in Gilead.

The Israelites sent twelve companies of soldiers to Jabesh-gilead. They soon returned, bringing four hundred young women with them.

Then they sent messengers to offer peace to the Benjaminites at the Rock of Rimmon. The six hundred men came out of hiding and returned to Shiloh with the messengers.

But there were only four hundred wives for six hundred men. Where could they find two hundred more wives?

Someone had another idea. It was almost time for one of the yearly festivals at Shiloh. They made plans for bold action.

The two hundred men without wives hid in the vineyards during the festival. When the young women of Shiloh came out to dance, the Benjaminites rushed forward and grabbed them. They kidnapped the dancers and carried them back as brides to their own land. They married them and rebuilt their cities and settled down to build up their tribe again.

The fathers of the girls complained, but the leaders of Israel told them that this was the only way to keep the tribe of Benjamin from dying out.

Crime, war between tribes, kidnapping—these were just some of the strange events that happened in the days of the judges. Whenever they

forgot the teaching of the Lord, the Israelites found themselves in trouble. When they worshiped the Lord, they served him as king and they loved each other. When they worshiped idols, they served foreign rulers and they fought among themselves.

A Redeemer for Naomi

Naomi's Bitter Return

Ruth 1

WHILE some people in Israel forgot the Lord and worshiped idols, others remembered him and his teaching. They loved the Lord and were kind to each other, and lived the way God wanted his people to live. God acted in their lives, making good things happen.

A man named Elimelech lived in the town of Bethlehem in the land of Judah in the days of the judges. Elimelech had a wife named Naomi and two sons called Mahlon and Chilion. For several years the weather was bad and crops were poor, so there wasn't enough food for everyone in Bethlehem. Because of this famine, Elimelech and his wife and boys went to live in the land of Moab, which was east of Judah, on the other side of the Salt Sea.

They stayed in Moab about ten years. During that time Elimelech died, and Naomi's two sons married Moabite women. One was named Orpah and the other was named Ruth. Then both Mahlon and Chilion died, leaving Naomi a widow with no sons.

One day Naomi heard that the Lord had blessed the people of Judah with good harvests. The famine was over. She thought at once of going home, and prepared to leave Moab alone. But as she was beginning her journey, Orpah and Ruth walked along the road beside her.

"Go back," Naomi told them. "Return home, both of you. May the Lord treat you with loving kindness, as you have treated me and my sons. May the Lord reward each of you with a new husband."

Then she kissed them both good-bye.

The two young women began to cry. "We don't want to leave you," they said to Naomi. "We'll go back with you to your native land and live with you and your people."

But Naomi said again, "Go back, my daughters. What's the use of coming with me? I don't have any more sons to take care of you. I'm too old to marry again, and even if I did, and had sons, would you wait for them to grow up? No, my daughters. Go back. Life is more bitter for me than for you. You're young enough to remarry and have sons, but I'm too old! There's no one left to take care of me. Surely, the hand of the Lord is raised against me!"

The two young women began to cry again.

Finally, Orpah dried her tears and kissed Naomi good-bye and went back to her own people.

But Ruth stayed with Naomi, holding on to her tightly.

"Now look, Ruth," said Naomi. "Your sister is going back to her people and her god. You go with her."

"Don't force me to go back and leave you alone!" said Ruth.

For wherever you go, I will go.
Wherever you stay, I will stay.
Your people will be my people.
Your God is now my God.
Wherever you die, I will die,
and there I will be buried.
May the Lord punish me
if even death should come between us!

At last Naomi realized that Ruth was determined to go with her, so she said no more. The two women walked along the road together, westward toward Bethlehem.

When they arrived in Bethlehem, the whole town hummed with excitment about Naomi's return. Her friends hadn't seen her for ten years.

"Is it really you, Naomi?" the women asked.

"Don't call me Naomi anymore," she answered. "That name means 'sweet.' Call me Mara, which means 'bitter.' For God Almighty has made me truly bitter.

I left Bethlehem
    full of happiness.
But the Lord has brought me back empty.
Why call me Naomi,
    for the Lord has accused me,
    and God Almighty has punished me!

With this bitter news, Naomi returned from the land of Moab with her daughter-in-law Ruth. They happened to arrive in the early spring, just in time for the grain harvest.

33

Ruth Gleans in the Field of Boaz

Ruth 2

THE fields around Bethlehem were full of ripe barley, ready to be cut and harvested. Later it would be ground into flour. During the harvest, men went out to the fields to cut the grain with short sickles. Women walked behind these reapers and tied the stalks of grain into bundles, or sheaves. Other workers loaded the sheaves onto the backs of donkeys and took the grain to the threshing floor. There they beat the stalks of grain to separate the kernels of grain from the straw.

According to the teaching of God in the law of Moses, poor people could go to the fields at harvesttime and gather any grain which was left on the ground. This was called gleaning.

Soon after they arrived in Bethlehem, Ruth said to Naomi, "I'm going out to the fields to find someone who will let me glean the barley which the reapers leave."

"Yes, go on, my daughter," answered Naomi.

Early the next morning Ruth walked out to the fields where the reapers were working and received permission from the foreman to glean. She came to the part of the fields which belonged to Boaz, a wealthy cousin of Elimelech.

That same morning Boaz himself happened to come out to the fields from Bethlehem.

"The Lord be with you!" he greeted his workers.

"The Lord bless you!" they answered.

Then Boaz noticed Ruth. "Who's that young woman?" he asked the man in charge of the reapers.

"She's a Moabite girl," the man answered. "She's the one who came back with Naomi. She asked if she could glean the barley after the reapers. She's been out here since early this morning."

Boaz went up to Ruth and spoke to her. He was an older man with a kind expression on his face.

"Listen to me, my daughter," he said. "Don't go to any other field to glean. Stay here with my servant girls. Keep your eyes on them and follow behind them. I'm ordering my servants not to bother you. If you get thirsty, go over there to the water jars and drink what they have brought."

Ruth bowed low before Boaz, so low that her face touched the ground. "Why have you noticed me, a foreigner?" she asked.

He answered, "I've heard about everything you've done for your mother-in-law since your husband's death. You left your native land and came to live among strangers for her sake. May the Lord reward you for what you've done! May the God of Israel, who protects all of us, give you shelter beneath his wings!"

Ruth answered, "You're very kind, sir. Your gentle words make me feel much better. I hope you continue to be pleased with me. I am at your service, sir, but, indeed, I'm far beneath your servants!"

When it was time to eat, Boaz said to Ruth, "Come here and share our lunch. Have some of this bread. Here, dip it into the wine."

Ruth sat down next to the reapers, and Boaz gave her a large portion of food. She ate until she was full, and she even had some left over.

When Ruth went back to work, Boaz ordered his servants, "Let this young woman glean among the sheaves. Don't bother her. And when you're reaping and binding the sheaves, pull out some of the stalks of grain from the bundles and let them fall to the ground in front of her."

Ruth worked all day, and when she was finished, she pounded out the stalks to separate the grain from the straw. She weighed it carefully. She had more then twenty-five pounds of barley! She took the grain home with her and showed it to Naomi.

Then she surprised her mother-in-law with the food she had saved from lunch.

"Where did you get all this grain?" asked Naomi. "Who has been so kind to you? Blessed be the man who noticed you!"

Ruth told her about Boaz.

"May the Lord bless him!" said Naomi. "The Lord is good and keeps his promises after all.

This man is related to my husband!"

Then she explained to Ruth that according to the law of Moses, the family of a dead man was supposed to support and protect the widow. To keep the man's property in the family and to carry on his name, the dead man's brother or nearest relative was supposed to marry the widow. The relative who took on this responsibility was called the "redeemer."

"There's more!" said Ruth when Naomi was finished talking. "Boaz told me to stay with his workers and glean in his field until the end of the harvest!"

"Yes," agreed Naomi, "it would be better for you to go with his servants than to some other field where someone might bother you."

So each morning Ruth went out to glean in the fields of Boaz. She stayed in his fields and worked behind his servants until the barley and the wheat were harvested.

34

Boaz at the Threshing Floor

Ruth 3

ONE day in late spring Naomi said to Ruth, "My daughter, I want to take care of you and see that you are settled. Tonight Boaz and his workers are celebrating the festival of the grain harvest. They're at the threshing floor near the city gate. Wash and put on perfume, dress in your best clothes, and go down there. Follow my directions, and do whatever Boaz tells you."

"Whatever you say," answered Ruth.

She went down to the threshing floor and did everything exactly as Naomi told her. She hid until Boaz was finished eating and drinking and his heart was merry. She waited while he settled down to sleep at the far end of the threshing floor, by the pile of barley.

Then she quietly went and turned back his cover and lay down at his feet.

In the middle of the night Boaz felt cold and reached for his cover. He sat up and looked around. Was that a woman lying at his feet?

"Who are you?" he asked.

"I'm Ruth, your servant. Spread your wing over me, and take me under your protection. You're one of our redeemers!"

Boaz understood what she meant. "May the Lord bless you!" he said. "First you were kind to Naomi by coming to Bethlehem. Now, instead of looking for a young man to marry, you're asking me! Don't be afraid. Everyone in Bethlehem knows that you're a wonderful young woman. Yes, it's true that I have the right of redemption, but there's another man who's a closer relative. Wait here tonight, and in the morning I'll speak to him. If he wants to be your redeemer, well, let him. But if not, why then, as the Lord lives, I'll redeem you myself!"

Ruth lay at Boaz' feet until morning, and then she got up before it was light enough for anyone to see her.

"Hold out your cloak," said Boaz, and he poured some barley into it for her and sent her back to town.

"What happened?" asked Naomi when she got home.

Ruth told her what Boaz had said. "He gave me these six measures of barley, and he told me, 'Don't go back empty-handed to your mother-in-law!'"

"Now let's just sit here and wait to see what happens," said Naomi. "Boaz won't rest until he settles the matter, and I think he'll settle it today!"

35

The Redeemer

Ruth 4

WHILE Naomi and Ruth waited at home, Boaz went up to the gate of the town, where the town business was conducted. He sat on the bench built into the open space inside the gate.

Just then, the relative he was looking for happened to come by.

"Come here, man," said Boaz. "Take a seat."

He came and sat down by Boaz.

Then Boaz picked out ten of the town leaders as they came through the gate. "Sit down here," he told them.

Boaz said to the man, "Elimelech's widow, Naomi, has returned from Moab. She's selling some land which belonged to our cousin, Elimelech. I want you to know, for you have the right to redeem the land now, in front of these men. If you don't want to, tell me, for I am the only other person who can do it. The land should stay in her family, but you're the closer relative, so you decide."

"I'm willing to redeem the land," said the man.

"Wait, there's more to tell," said Boaz. "If you buy the field, you're responsible for Naomi's daughter-in-law, Ruth, who is also a widow. You must marry her, so the property will stay in Elimelech's family and the family name won't die out."

"If that's so," said the man, "I can't do it, for I have enough responsibilities. You redeem her yourself."

"Look!" said Boaz to the people at the gate, "You're witnesses today. I'm buying what belonged to Elimelech and his sons. And, more important, I'm taking responsibility for Ruth, the widow of Mahlon. I'm going to marry her and keep his name alive among our people!"

"We're witnesses!" said all the people at the gate.

Then the leaders of the town blessed Boaz and Ruth. "May the Lord give Ruth many children to build up your family! May they make a name for you in Bethlehem!"

Boaz and Ruth were married, and the Lord gave them a son.

Naomi's friends came to celebrate with her. "Praise the Lord!" they said. "Today he has given you a redeemer, to keep your husband's name alive in Israel! He has made your life sweet again. This child will take care of you when you're old. Your daughter-in-law, who loves you, is worth more to you than seven sons."

Naomi took the boy and held him in her arms.

"A son has been born for Naomi," said the neighbor women, and they named him Obed.

Because Naomi and Ruth and Boaz loved God and each other, the Lord did great things through their family. Obed grew up and had a son named Jesse, and Jesse had a son named David, who was God's chosen king of Israel.

THE WORLD OF JOSHUA, JUDGES, AND RUTH

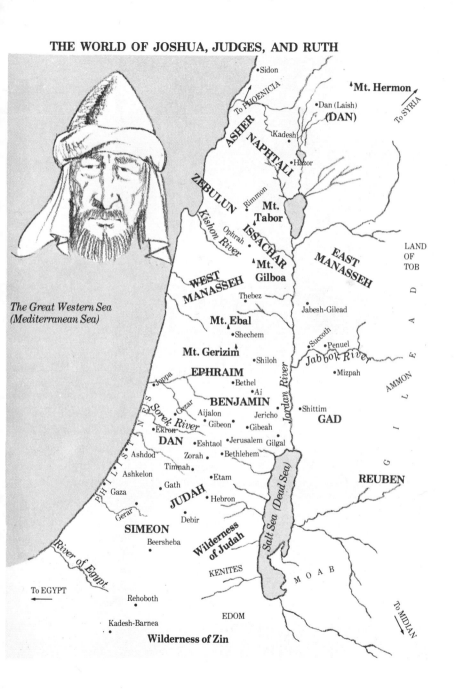

Sidon

Mt. Hermon

To SYRIA

To PHOENICIA

Dan (Laish)
(DAN)

ASHER

Kadesh

NAPHTALI

Hazor

ZEBULUN

Rimmon

Mt. Tabor

Kishon River

Ophrah

ISSACHAR

EAST MANASSEH

LAND OF TOB

WEST MANASSEH

Mt. Gilboa

The Great Western Sea (Mediterranean Sea)

Thebez

Jabesh-Gilead

Mt. Ebal

Shechem

Succoth

Penuel

Mt. Gerizim

Shiloh

Jabbok River

EPHRAIM

Bethel

Ai

Mizpah

Joppa

Gezer

BENJAMIN

Aijalon

Jericho

Shittim

AMMON

Sorek River

Gibeon

Gibeah

GAD

Ekron

DAN

Eshtaol

Jerusalem

Gilgal

Ashdod

Zorah

Bethlehem

Ashkelon

Timnah

Gaza

Gath

Etam

REUBEN

Hebron

JUDAH

Debir

Gerar

SIMEON

Beersheba

Wilderness of Judah

KENITES

River of Egypt

To EGYPT

Rehoboth

EDOM

Kadesh-Barnea

Wilderness of Zin

Salt Sea (Dead Sea)

Jordan River

G I L E A D

M O A B

To MIDIAN

Eve Bowers MacMaster graduated from the Pennsylvania State University and George Washington University. She also studied at Harvard University and Eastern Mennonite Seminary. She has taught in the Bible department at Eastern Mennonite College and in the history department at James Madison University, both located in Harrisonburg, Virginia.

Eve visited many of the places mentioned in the Bible while she was serving as a Peace Corps Volunteer in Turkey.

Eve and her husband, Richard, live near Harrisonburg, Virginia, with their children, Sam, Tom, and Sarah.